Official Cambridge Exam Preparation

COMPLETE

ADVANCED

**Workbook
with answers
with eBook**

Third edition

C1

Claire Wijayatilake

Shaftesbury Road, Cambridge CB2 8EA, United Kingdom

One Liberty Plaza, 20th Floor, New York, NY 10006, USA

477 Williamstown Road, Port Melbourne, VIC 3207, Australia

314–321, 3rd Floor, Plot 3, Splendor Forum, Jasola District Centre, New Delhi – 110025, India

103 Penang Road, #05–06/07, Visioncrest Commercial, Singapore 238467

Cambridge University Press & Assessment is a department of the University of Cambridge.

We share the University's mission to contribute to society through the pursuit of education, learning and research at the highest international levels of excellence.

www.cambridge.org
Information on this title: www.cambridge.org/9781009162340

© Cambridge University Press & Assessment 2009, 2014, 2023

First published 2009
Second edition 2014
Third edition 2023

20 19 18 17 16 15 14 13 12 11 10 9 8 7

Printed in Dubai by Oriental Press

A catalogue record for this publication is available from the British Library

ISBN 978-1-009-16234-0 Workbook with Answers with eBook

Additional resources for this publication at www.cambridge.org/complete

Contents

1 People like us

Grammar

Verb forms to talk about the past

1 Circle the correct alternative in *italics* to complete the text.

When I **(1)** *was growing up / grew up*, my parents
(2) *would be / were* very protective of me. They
(3) *have had / had* me when they were older and
(4) *had always wanted / have always been wanting* a
daughter. When I was a young child, I **(5)** *was loving /
loved* being an only child as I **(6)** *got / had been getting*
all my parents' attention. When I became a teenager,
my parents realised they **(7)** *had been spoiling /
were spoiling* me for too long and I **(8)** *became /
had become* rather self-centred. I've got children of my
own now. Since they **(9)** *had been / were* born, I
(10) *have been trying / had been trying* hard not to
spoil them
because I
want them to
grow up into
thoughtful and
considerate
adults.

2 Find and correct the errors in six of these sentences.

1 My grandfather used to be very open-minded but
he's changed as he's got older.
2 When I was walking down the high street on
Saturday, I had bumped into a girl I was at
school with.
3 Yesterday was a school day so what have you been
doing hanging round in the park at 10 o'clock
in the morning?
4 My brother would be a faster runner than me but
nowadays I can run much faster than he can.
5 I used to hate going to visit my cousins because they
would wind me up all the time.
6 When Marlena finally turned up, we have been
waiting for over an hour.
7 Rafi was an imaginative child; he had been always
thinking up stories.
8 I think I'm losing my voice. I talked all day.

3 Complete the sentences with the correct past form
of the verbs in brackets.

1 When my grandmother was growing up, she
.... (has) to do without luxuries because
her family .... (be) very poor.
2 Jason .... (fall) apart when he heard that
he .... (fail) all his exams.
3 Every Sunday in the summer when I was a child, we
.... (pack) up a picnic and .... (go)
off into the countryside on our bikes.
4 What .... (happen) when I called you last
night? Your dog .... (bark)
so loudly!
5 Simon .... (not work) there long when
Grace .... (join) the company.
6 Sorry I look such a mess. I .... (garden)
all afternoon.
7 I .... (be) excited to meet Miranda last
week as I .... (never meet) anyone so
unconventional before.
8 Dylan .... (manage) to catch up with
all his friends before he .... (head)
off to Australia.

Vocabulary

Collocations with *give* and *make*

1 Complete the sentences with the correct form of
give or *make*.

1 You seem to have .... a good impression
on Mr Cullen – he wants to offer you the job.
2 We like to .... our students the
opportunity to go on a school trip at least once
a year.
3 When I was young, my parents .... me lots
of good advice but I didn't always take it.
4 Would you mind .... me more details
about the club and how I could join it?
5 I'm lucky that my parents always .... time
to play with my brother and me.
6 Both reports and proposals usually involve
.... recommendations.
7 This Thursday, the police will be coming to school to
.... a talk about online safety.
8 Unfortunately, I can't go to the concert tonight. I
hope they'll .... me my money back.

2 Complete the phrases 1–8 with *give* or *make*. Then match the phrases to the correct definitions A–H.

1 .... an apology
2 .... (someone) a refund/their money back
3 .... a lecture
4 .... (someone) some information/details
5 .... a phone call
6 .... a suggestion
7 .... a comment
8 .... (someone) instructions

A tell someone some facts
B say you are sorry
C remark on something
D teach a large group of students at university
E tell someone how to do something
F return some money to someone
G put forward an idea for consideration
H contact someone by phone

Reading and Use of English Part 4

In Part 4, you often have to identify a 'chunk' of language, such as a fixed phrase, dependent preposition or phrasal verb, as well as making grammatical changes – remember that two different changes are needed for each question.
Exam advice

For questions 1–6, complete the second sentence so that it has a similar meaning to the first sentence, using the word given. Do not change the word given. You must use between three and six words, including the word given.

1 Local volunteers deliver the newsletter every week.
BASIS
The newsletter
.... by
local volunteers.

2 Jo suggested making the exam longer.
INCREASE
Jo said it would be a good idea
.... of
the exam.

3 Sue was visiting her great-aunt for the first time.
PAID
Sue .... her
great-aunt before.

4 It's fine to borrow money occasionally
HARM
There's ....
a loan from time to time.

5 People have fewer children than they did in the past.
MANY
People .... as
they used to.

6 He can't be allowed to continue to behave so badly.
STOP
We have .... to
his bad behaviour.

Listening Part 4

When you choose between the options for a speaker, remember that some options may seem quite tempting when you listen, but only one option in each task will be correct for that speaker.

Exam advice

 You will hear five short extracts in which people are talking about someone they admire.

TASK ONE
For questions 1-5, choose from the list (A-H) the qualities each speaker believes the person they admire has.

A being determined and hard-working
B being fun and sociable
C being unconventional and open-minded
D being analytical and a problem-solver
E being persuasive and self-assured
F being rational and sensible
G being calm and self-aware
H being exciting and adventurous

Speaker 1		1		Speaker 4		4
Speaker 2		2		Speaker 5		5
Speaker 3		3				

TASK TWO
For questions 6-10, choose from the list (A-H) what change the speaker made as a result of this person's influence.

A starting a business
B clearing their debts
C taking up a new activity
D changing profession
E acquiring self-belief
F gaining a qualification
G improving their social life
H stopping judging people

Speaker 1		6		Speaker 4		9
Speaker 2		7		Speaker 5		10
Speaker 3		8				

Reading and Use of English Part 8

You are going to read four reviews of a book about friendship which is aimed at young adults. For questions (1–10), choose from the reviews A–D. The reviews may be chosen more than once.

The words used in the questions will not be the same as those in the text: look out for synonyms and antonyms as well as paraphrases of the ideas in the questions.

Exam advice

Which reviewer

1   disagrees with the author on a cause of problems in relationships?

2   questions the author's understanding of the complexity of relationships?

3   admits they don't always pay their full attention when someone speaks?

4   realises that their interactions with friends often lacked depth?

5   refers to a specific case when not being aware of a friend's situation caused a problem?

6   appreciates the author's attitude to occasionally putting one's own interests first?

7   writes positively about the value of the book's visual aspects?

8   was surprised by how an action recommended in the book was received?

9   mentions someone who was concerned about others' behaviour?

10 doubts the reliability of some of the accounts in the book?

Make new friends...but keep the old - *four book reviews*

A

Everyone was raving about this book, so I finally got myself a copy. Having read it from cover to cover, I am still in two minds about it. To my way of thinking, it oversimplifies relationships and seems to imply that if you do X, then Y will happen, which is not necessarily the case. It included some sweeping generalisations about males and females and how they operate within friendships, which I find difficult to accept. On the other hand, it did do me good to reflect on how I handle conflict with the people close to me and some parts of it were thought-provoking, particularly the part about setting boundaries. I thought it was selfish to refuse to do certain things for my friends, but now I realise that boundaries are an important part of self-care. It is refreshing to be told that doing something for yourself is a positive not a negative.

B

This book was recommended to our class by our deputy head teacher, who warned that some of us didn't know where to draw the line between friendly banter and bullying. It made me think differently about how I interact with my mates; for example, like many people, I'm guilty of selective listening, which can be detrimental to friendships. What the book has to say about the distractions of technology also rang a bell with me, because often we don't take notice of what our friends are saying or maintain eye-contact because we're too busy checking social media. There was a story in the book about a girl who was on the verge of dropping out of school because she was being bullied but her so-called friends didn't even realise what was going on. It highlighted the need to be more observant and proactive with friends rather than just reacting to what they tell us. Another thing I have taken away is the need to be spontaneous and touch base with friends just to show them I'm there for them.

C

I don't think I'd ever paid a compliment to any of my peers because I'd assumed I'd just be ridiculed. So, the other day I told my friend I liked his new haircut and he was actually pleased! This is just one of the effects this book had on me. What I liked most about it were the suggested 'tasks' – like paying a compliment to someone – things which don't take much effort but have a massive impact. I realised that I have often taken my friends for granted and assumed they'd be there in my time of need, but I didn't put much effort into the relationships. Most communication between us was superficial – either we'd be talking about trivial things or we were complaining endlessly about homework and exams. I didn't realise the importance of showing appreciation for the people we care about or the effect meaningful friendships can have on one's overall well-being. Personally, I'd lose the pictures, though – they are cute but a bit of a distraction.

D

I can't quite make up my mind about this book, but then I'm still only about two thirds of the way through it. What I love is that it seems very inclusive, and the writer seems to value diversity. Having said that, there are a few parts I find quite irritating. Whilst the author is well aware of the fact that relationships can be complicated, I can't subscribe to the assumption that every emotional issue inevitably stems from our childhood. It doesn't necessarily follow that a difficult start in life leads to less harmonious relationships in adulthood. Some of the examples seem a touch contrived and I question whether they are based on actual people. I'd have preferred a more scientific approach with deeper insights to explore some of the more intricate relationships that are mentioned in the book. The illustrations, while not strictly necessary in a book aimed at this age group, really cheered me up!

Writing Part 1

An essay

1 Read the exam task below. Say *Yes* or *No* to the following statements.

1 You should give your views on all three of the ideas.   Yes / No

2 You must choose which of the two ideas you feel is the best choice.   Yes / No

3 You must refer to at least one of the opinions in the task.   Yes / No

4 When referring to the opinions, you should paraphrase.   Yes / No

5 You should write as much as you possibly can.   Yes / No

Exam advice

As well as your content and language, you will be marked on your organisation: ensure you have a clear introduction and conclusion as well as a separate paragraph for each of the two items you discuss.

Your class has attended a panel discussion in the Town Hall about who should be chosen as your town's 'Person of the Year'. You have made the notes below:

Ideas for Person of the Year

- A local politician
- A teacher
- A sportsperson

Some opinions expressed in the discussion:

'Politicians divide public opinion.'

'The work of teachers is important to everyone.'

'Sports people bring fame to our town.'

Write an **essay** discussing **two** of the types of people who could be chosen for Person of the Year. You should **explain which you feel is more suitable**, giving **reasons** to support your opinion.

You may, if you wish, make use of the opinions expressed in the discussion, but you should use your own words as far as possible.

Write your answer in 220-260 words in an appropriate style.

2 Read the essay written by an exam candidate who completed this Part 1 task. Then complete it using the linking words and phrases from the box below. Some words can be used in more than one space.

> although   despite   firstly   however   in this way
> moreover   nevertheless   on the other hand   secondly   since

'Person of the Year' is a prestigious award given to someone from our town every year. It's always a difficult choice to make. So many make a valuable contribution to our community. **(1)** .... , we can only recognise one with this award. I would like to give my views on two of the types of people the town could honour **(2)** .... : a teacher and a sportsperson.

(3) .... , let's consider teachers. 'Ordinary' citizens such as these are often overlooked for awards of this type, **(4)** .... the vital work they do in our communities. On the one hand, we should definitely show our appreciation for their role in our lives. **(5)** .... , it would be difficult to choose just one teacher as the recipient of the award, **(6)** .... they all work so hard on our behalf.

(7) .... , I would like to consider the pros and cons of choosing a sportsperson. On the positive side, the well-known sportsmen and women from our town are an inspiration to young people. **(8)** .... , they have given us all something to celebrate and put our small town on the map. **(9)** .... , those who excel in sports have already been rewarded for their efforts with trophies, medals and celebrity.

Having considered these two groups of people, my personal view is that the award should go to a sportsperson. **(10)** .... teachers definitely deserve our appreciation and respect, I feel it would be difficult to single out just one to receive this accolade.

3 Read the model essay again. Has the writer:

1 written within the word limit?   Yes / No

2 discussed two of the ideas?   Yes / No

3 given their opinion on which is the most suitable?   Yes / No

4 organised their writing into paragraphs?   Yes / No

5 used a wide range of vocabulary and sentence structure?   Yes / No

2 More than words

Vocabulary

Collocations with *make*, *get* and *do*

1 Circle the correct alternative in italics to complete the sentences.

1 I *got / made* the impression that Charlotte was just putting a brave face on things.
2 It never *does / makes* any harm to overprepare for an exam.
3 We don't often *make / get* many customer complaints, but when we do, we try to solve the problem straightaway.
4 Don't be nervous about your speaking test: just relax and *make / do* your best.
5 Good communicators always *make / get* a point of listening carefully to the other person.
6 Some students don't want to learn a language because they don't think they'll ever get a chance to *get / make* use of it.
7 What kind of speaking activities do you *make / do* in your English class?
8 The problem with having a desk job is you often don't *get / make* enough exercise.
9 Your speaking won't improve unless you *do / make* an effort to practise.
10 I rarely feel like *making / doing* the cooking when I get home from work.

2 Complete the sentences with the correct form of *make*, *get* or *do*.

1 I don't enjoy .... household chores so I spend as little time as possible on them.
2 The proposal .... on behalf of the council for extra funding has been denied.
3 I know it was a difficult decision, but I think you .... the right choice in the end.
4 Layla's English is almost fluent but she still .... mistakes with tenses.
5 The headteacher has decided to .... changes to the way the children are taught basic skills.
6 First, you need to .... some qualifications; then you can start looking for a job.
7 Miguel finds it easy to .... friends; it's his brother I'm worried about.
8 My mum asked me to .... some shopping for her on my way home from school.
9 Slow down! You're not .... any sense. Say it again.
10 After school, I'm hoping to .... a course in filmmaking.

Grammar

Expressing purpose, reason and result

1 Complete the blog post with a linking expression from the box.

> as a consequence of   in order to   since   in case
> so as   therefore   for the purpose of   this reason

Several social media platforms have been created **(1)** .... allowing people to communicate a message within a very short time. Teenagers and young adults are used to a fast-paced world. **(2)** For ...., they are the target audience for these sites. **(3)** .... most older people prefer communicating more carefully and at a slower pace, they are less likely to engage with this kind of platform. **(4)** .... young people are free to express themselves without their elders observing them. This is a desirable situation for many adolescents **(5)** .... to avoid judgment and criticism. However, child protection experts say online communication should always be monitored **(6)** .... bullying occurs. Many people believe that age limits on social media sites should be more strictly enforced **(7)** .... protect vulnerable young people. **(8)** .... such limits, children will be able to enjoy a stress-free childhood.

2 Join the two sentences using the linking expression in brackets. Make any other necessary changes.

1 Let's turn the subtitles on. We might not understand everything. (in case)
....
2 We took lots of photos on holiday. We can remember the good times. (so that)
....
3 Leon hasn't spoken French for several years. His French is a bit rusty. (As)
....
4 Samira lived in Greece as a child. She speaks Greek really well. (with the result that)
....
5 The lecture was cancelled. The lecturer was ill. (due to)
....
6 The school reduced the fees. They got more students. (with the intention of)
....

Listening Part 1

In Listening Part 1, you will be tested on your ability to understand gist, detail, function, agreement and course of action, as well as the speakers' purpose, feelings, attitudes and opinions. Mark one option after the first listening and use the second to check your answer.

Exam advice

You will hear three different extracts. For questions 1–6, choose the answer (A, B or C) that fits best according to what you hear. There are two questions for each extract.

Extract 1

You hear two friends discussing a TV documentary about how babies learn to speak.

1 What information given in the documentary does the man find hard to believe?

A that one-year-old babies only produce the sounds of their carers' language

B that the ability to learn languages is present in infants from birth

C that newborns are able to make out and produce sounds from every language

2 The woman says that she learnt that

A there is a great deal of variance in babies' rate of development.

B patterns of acquisition do not vary according to mother tongue.

C speaking to babies helps speed up the learning process.

Extract 2

You hear two friends talking about a language speaking test in schools.

3 The man disagrees with the woman's view about the speaking test because he thinks

A she has misunderstood the planned alterations.

B examiners are best placed to grade students' speaking.

C preparing for an exam takes time away from teaching.

4 What is the woman's opinion on learning languages in school?

A Pupils will be less motivated if it is made compulsory.

B Children should study a language even if they don't want to.

C Schools need to change how students view languages.

Extract 3

You hear a man talking to a woman about a text message he has received from his daughter.

5 Why does the woman dismiss the man's complaint about his daughter's text message?

A She feels he should learn the abbreviations she uses.

B She doesn't mind not understanding young people.

C She understands that language change is normal.

6 Why does the woman mention a pram?

A to show that languages change for users' convenience.

B to illustrate the rates of change of spoken and written language.

C to give an example of the language from a historical period.

Reading and Use of English Part 3

Read the words around the gaps carefully and decide what kind of word is missing. Remember, a prefix might be needed so that the word makes sense in the context.

Exam advice

For questions 1–8, read the text below. Use the word given in capitals at the end of some of the lines to form a word that fits in the gap in the same line. There is an example at the beginning (0).

Example (0): BELOVED

Communicating with our pets	
Many of us want to be able to interact with our **(0)** BELOVED pets, but one woman from Washington has taught her dog Bunny to communicate in a rather	LOVE
(1) .... way. Alexis Devine created a 'language machine' using sound buzzers to enable Bunny to talk to her. After many hours of	CONVENTION
(2) .... practice, Bunny can tell her precisely what he needs.	REPEAT
Many pet experts believe we **(3)** .... our pets' abilities. Some cite the example of Rico, a border collie who could	ESTIMATE
(4) .... between the words for 200 objects. There are others, however, who claim the cases of Bunny and Rico are	DIFFERENT
(5) ...., as they insist animals can be taught to understand our languages.	LEAD
What is beyond doubt is that both dogs and cats find ways to communicate with their owners. A cat's whiskers pulled against its cheeks, for example, is an	
(6) .... of fear, while half-closing the eyes shows	INDICATE
(7) .... Instead of inventing complicated machines, most pet lovers simply need to	CONTENT
raise their **(8)** .... of their pet's body language.	AWARE

2

Writing Part 2

A report

1 Read the exam task below.

> The developers of a new language learning app, Linguamundo, have invited you to take part in a trial to study two languages: English at Advanced level and a new language at Beginner level.
>
> You have been asked to write a report about your experiences with the app. Your report should evaluate the app's value for both Beginners and Advanced learners and suggest ways it could be improved.
>
> **Write your report in 220–260 words.**

2 Answer the questions.

1 Who is the report for?
2 Which three verbs in the second paragraph give instructions for the task?
3 What is the purpose of the report?

> Reports are usually divided into sections with headings. Start with the purpose of the report. Make sure to cover all the points in the question. Most reports end with recommendations.
>
> **Exam advice**

3 Read the report written by an exam candidate. Choose a heading for each section. There are three extra headings.

> The free app   The premium version
> Introduction   Recommendations
> Good points of the app   Development of the app
> Points to improve   General evaluation

1 [ ]

I recently spent two weeks trialling the Linguamundo app. As an advanced learner of English, I used the premium Advanced add-on, while also using the free app to begin learning German. The aim of this report is to share my personal experiences of using the app.

2 [ ]

Both the basic programme and the Advanced add-on were attractive, enjoyable to use and effective. As a learner, I made outstanding progress in both languages. However, both versions could benefit from further development.

3 [ ]

Having had no previous exposure to the German language, I was astonished by how quickly I was able to grasp the basics. The colourful and entertaining visuals enhanced my experience and made the new words and phrases more memorable. There are still a few bugs, though, and occasionally the app shuts down mid-exercise.

4 [ ]

Advanced learners of any language need to pay to use the app. This is, in my view, reasonable, given the work that goes into preparing materials at a higher level. While vocabulary and grammar lessons were useful and engaging, the app does not really focus on skills development. Links to reading and listening materials were provided; however, these were disappointing as there were no tasks to aid comprehension.

5 [ ]

There are three suggestions I would like to make. The first would be to add a few more languages, in addition to the five already provided; Mandarin, Japanese and Arabic would be the most useful. Secondly, extend the Advanced level to the other core languages. And lastly, further develop the skills-based materials to enable advanced learners to practise their reading and listening skills.

4 Read the report again. Which adjectives does the writer use to describe the following?

1 The app in general ....
2 Her progress in both languages while using the app generally

....

3 Her reaction to her own progress in German

....

4 The visuals ....
5 The fact that advanced learners have to pay

....

6 The advanced grammar and vocabulary lessons

....

7 The reading and listening materials

....

Reading and Use of English Part 6

You are going to read four extracts from articles written by people who have experienced remote working. For questions 1–4, choose from the extracts **A–D**. The extracts may be chosen more than once.

Which writer

1 has a different view from the others on the effect of remote working on work-life balance?

2 shares A's view on how enjoyable remote working is?

3 has a similar view to B on how remote working influences work relationships?

4 has a different opinion from D on the consequences for managers of remote working?

Remote working

A One of the main benefits of remote working has been its effect on home life. Those who had long commutes or spend a long time in the office rarely shared a meal with their families. Now, they have ample time to do so. The increase in family time can only be a positive impact. I would also argue that work itself is proving more pleasurable for most people as a result of the move to remote working. And managers, as I see it, are reaping the rewards: By giving employees more independence and flexibility to manage their workloads, they've found themselves with a more empowered and motivated workforce. It would seem that the more autocratic approach to management is a thing of the past. It's not all plain sailing, though. For people who live alone, the isolation from supportive colleagues can be extremely challenging.

B There's a lot to be said for remote working. It's striking to see the increased number of businesses promoting it. Many have realised it's an incentive that can attract good people to their companies. Some are even offering to cover the cost of utility bills, which I feel is a step in the right direction. The important question is though, when our office and personal space are indistinguishable, can we ever truly switch off from work? It's tempting, and understandably so, for workers to check an extra email or finalise a report when the computer is just there, but the prospect of longer hours and increased stress makes the threat of burnout all too real. This is compounded by the absence of co-workers with whom one can vent one's frustrations, often a major benefit of workplace life. To ensure that employee well-being is maintained, it's something that managers are going to have to keep a close eye on.

C When it comes to making remote working a success, there's one key factor that mustn't be overlooked: trust. There's an old saying 'out of sight, out of mind' and it's one that I feel bosses are all too aware of, even fearful of. No longer being able to poke their heads round the door or glance up from the desks to see how staff are working, they're overcompensating; setting up a seemingly endless number of meetings and drop-in sessions to find out what their employees are up to or whether they're at their virtual desks. This is counter-productive, in my view, and something that could negatively impact on worker motivation, well-being and productivity – three things remote working should, in theory, help to improve. There is some evidence, however, that the physical distance from one's colleagues may actually be beneficial to mental well-being as workers no longer need to invest mental energy in interactions with people they haven't chosen to be with.

D One of the main attractions of remote working is putting a distance between the individual and those sometimes toxic office 'friendships' which sap one's energy. Being able to take care of home and garden during the day and thinking about something other than work during breaks, in my view, makes for a less stressful life. Now that remote working is almost the norm, managers have realised no-one has reduced their output, which has resulted in a more 'hands off' leadership style. I assume that most experienced employees find working without distractions has helped them rediscover the joy and satisfaction of a job well done. However, newer members of staff might find the lack of supervision a little nerve-wracking. The need to have excellent internet connectivity has caused many companies to pay for their staff's home Wi-Fi, saving them money. This is in addition to the money saved by not commuting to the office every day.

3 Mind, body and soul

Vocabulary

Multi-word verbs

1 Replace the words in italics with the correct form of a multi-word verb from the box. There is one multi-word verb that you don't need to use.

> catch on   come across as   come up   do away with
> get into   put forward   rush into
> settle down   take on

1 I'm happy that the school has *abolished* intelligence tests for 11-year-old pupils.
2 David has been studying psychology for a couple of months now and he's really *becoming interested* in it.
3 I bought a lottery ticket this morning and I really hope my numbers *are selected*.
4 Marta *seems* a bit serious but she's great fun once you get to know her.
5 Make sure you don't *agree to do* too much – everyone needs some free time.
6 People who *hurry into* marriage are less likely to be happy.
7 Charlotte *made* some very interesting suggestions at our last meeting.
8 A few of the kids at school have started wearing odd socks. I don't think it'll *become a trend*!

Verb collocations

2 Complete the sentences with the correct form of the words in the table. Use one word from column A and one word from column B in each sentence.

Column A	Column B
catch (x2)	as
make (x2)	eye
run	meet
take (x2)	point
	problems
	time
	with

1 Mia left home before me but I managed .... up .... her before she got to the bus stop.
2 We're not in any rush so let's .... our .... and get a coffee.
3 I'd always wanted a diamond engagement ring but when I saw the emerald one, it really .... my ....
4 My grandmother had seven children and she found it difficult to .... ends ....
5 When we were young, my parents always .... a .... of buying my sister and I the same number of presents.
6 My philosophy is to .... things .... they come – there's no point in worrying.
7 The developers .... into a lot of .... when it came to testing their latest software because they realised the coding was incorrect.

3 Replace the word or phrase in italics with a collocation from Exercise 2 in the correct form. Make any other changes necessary.

1 Maria hadn't decided what type of painting to buy – she just looked around until something *attracted her*.
2 Due to the recession, more and more families are struggling to *buy everything they need*.
3 Duncan did really well in the first part of the exam but he *had difficulty* with the second part.
4 Tabitha fell over at the start of the race but she managed to *reach* the other runners by the end of the first lap.
5 When I go to the supermarket, I always *remember to* buy some food for a needy family.
6 There's at least an hour till we need to be at the departure gate- you *don't need to hurry* in the duty-free shop.
7 Adam is a very relaxed kind of person – he just *accepts whatever happens*.

Grammar

no, none, not

1 Complete the dialogues with *no*, *none* or *not* in each gap.

1

A: There's **(1)** .... way I'd tell Brenda anything I didn't want anyone else to know.

B: Well, to be fair, **(2)** .... of your friends can keep a secret.

A: Mm, apart from Maxine, perhaps. She tends **(3)** .... to talk about other people.

2

A: I've had absolutely **(4)** .... food today. **(5)** .... that I was particularly hungry …

B: Why didn't you have a cake when the rest of us had one?

A: I was going to but there were **(6)** .... that I fancied.

3

A: Surely **(7)** .... everyone who likes green can be sincere and caring.

B: That's true. To be honest, I have **(8)** .... belief in that kind of generalisation.

A: Nor do I. **(9)** .... of those quizzes are ever accurate for me.

B: Well, they're just a bit of fun. There's **(10)** .... point taking them seriously.

The passive

2 Look at these sentences written by exam candidates. Some of them contain mistakes in the passive or active form. Find the mistake in each sentence and correct it or put a tick if the sentence is correct.

1 It has been reporting that girls and boys now perform equally well in Maths and Science.

2 The education system has been criticised for valuing certain types of intelligence more than others.

3 Experts still disagree about whether environmental factors or genetics have a greater influence on personality.

4 Evidence was currently being reviewed which suggests that intelligence is inherited from the mother, not the father.

5 A child's position in the family is strongly influenced by his or her character.

6 Not everyone believes that your favourite colour can reveal your personality.

7 The importance of interacting with babies cannot underestimated.

8 Emotional intelligence has being shown to be crucial to success at work.

9 Most people are still thought that the school you go to makes a difference to your educational achievement

10 Tests have been being carried out to determine the cause of the injury.

11 You can be found errors in the test results if you look carefully.

12 The report will have been published by the end of the year.

3 Complete the text with the correct form of the verbs in brackets. Decide whether the verb should be active or passive.

At school, children **(1)** .... (judge) according to a narrow definition of intelligence. They **(2)** .... (give) tests based on verbal (language-based) and non-verbal (recognition of patterns) intelligence. This approach to assessing intelligence is controversial because as we all **(3)** .... (know), there are many other types of intelligence, too. Some children **(4)** .... (excel) in creative subjects, such as art or music, while others possess a high degree of empathy. Unfortunately, these gifts **(5)** .... (overlook) in the kind of tests used to predict pupils' success at school. It **(6)** .... (show) that while intelligence tests have a limited role to play in assessing pupils' abilities, they do not reveal the complete picture. Children of average intelligence who **(7)** .... (nurture) at home, for instance, will usually do much better than predicted. Similarly, a child who possesses a positive attitude and work ethic **(8)** .... (have) an excellent chance of success. Interestingly, some education systems **(9)** .... (abandon) intelligence tests completely, whereas in others, they **(10)** .... (use) to this day.

Listening Part 2

You will hear a psychologist called Meera Khan talking about the rise in scamming where people are tricked by others who are trying to make a profit through deception. Complete the sentences with a word or short phrase.

1 Meera reveals that complaints about scams have increased by .... in recent years.

2 Meera talks about a woman called Amy whose tickets for a .... turned out to be a scam.

3 Meera gives an example of a couple whose fake website was used to sell .... to people.

4 Meera talks about a man called William who was tricked into paying for a .... at a non-existent company.

5 Meera suggests people avoid paying by .... when shopping online.

6 One sign that someone might not be genuine is a reluctance to have a .... with the person they've contacted through a dating website.

7 Meera refers back to the fake government website as an example of when having .... can put people at risk.

8 In Meera's opinion, ... are the best place to teach children to avoid being scammed.

Reading and Use of English Part 2

Exam advice

The missing words tend to be prepositions, conjunctions, determiners, auxiliary verbs, pronouns, etc. Some gaps can be filled by reading only the sentence, whereas for others, you will need to refer to the rest of the text.

Read the text below and think of the word which best fits each gap. Use only one word in each gap. There is an example at the beginning (0).

Example (0): most

The paradox of choice

Modern industrial societies promote the view that choice equals freedom, and for the **(0)** ....most........ part, that is true. According to psychologist, Barry Schwartz, **(1)** .... is in doubt is the belief that if some choice is good, more choice must be better.

Choice abounds in every part of our lives: from which product to buy to whether to get married. According to Schwartz, this over-abundance of choice is partly **(2)** .... blame for the fact that depression and feelings of inadequacy are **(3)** .... the rise. Multiple options offer people little or **(4)** .... benefit in terms of overall quality of life. Companies have **(5)** .... note of this: some major supermarkets have decided to reduce the number of options available, as it is more profitable to do **(6)** ...., reducing customer confusion in the process.

(7) .... of lower prices and better service, it led to anxiety and consumer inactivity. In many areas of life, it seems that having a choice can sometimes cause more difficulties than having **(8)** ....

Writing part 1

An essay

Your class has listened to a podcast about how to encourage people to adopt a healthy lifestyle.

Ways to persuade people to adopt a healthy lifestyle.

- Taxing unhealthy food
- Education programmes
- Celebrity endorsements

Some opinions expressed in the discussion.
'We should hit them where it hurts most – their pockets!'
'Children should learn about healthy lifestyles at school.'
'Most people want to be like the famous people they admire.'

Write an essay discussing two of the methods in your notes. You should say which method you feel would be more successful, giving reasons in support of your answer.

You may, if you wish, make use of the opinions expressed in the discussion, but you should use your own words as far as possible.

1 **Read this essay written by a student and then answer the questions.**

1 In which part of the essay does the writer introduce their own opinion?
2 In paragraph 2, the writer mentions a negative point about the method being discussed. How do they avoid presenting this as their own opinion?
3 In paragraph 3, does the writer present a negative point about the method being discussed? If so, what is it?

2 **Find the following in the essay:**

1 An example of emphasis
2 An adverb/verb collocation
3 An adverb used to express specific details of something you just mentioned
4 Two synonyms for 'encourage'
5 Two examples of the passive voice
6 Three words or phrases which introduce a contrast

3 **What do the underlined words and phrases refer to?**

1 so ....
2 their ....
3 the desired effect ....
4 the two methods discussed ....
5 one ....
6 those ....

Essay: What is the most effective way to encourage people to adopt a healthy lifestyle?

We all know that we should try and be healthier in our lifestyle choices – from exercising more to getting plenty of sleep and eating more fruit and vegetables. But what we disagree on is how best to convince others to make changes to their lifestyle. In this essay, I will consider two possibilities, namely taxing unhealthy food and celebrity endorsements.

Governments have the option to tax food and drink that are high in fat, salt or sugar, and several have already done <u>so</u>. On the one hand, this may result in some people choosing healthier products, in order to save money. However, one could also argue that it is unfair to make the lives of the disadvantaged even harder by denying them the pleasure of the food they choose to eat and drink.

One way that healthy lifestyles could be encouraged is by using celebrities to share information about how they keep themselves healthy through different types of media. People of all ages admire a range of sportsmen and women, film stars and singers, and <u>their</u> behaviour can strongly influence ours. It is important, though, that they are seen to do activities and use products that are accessible to everyone, if this is to have <u>the desired effect</u>.

In conclusion, my opinion is that of <u>the two methods discussed</u>, celebrity endorsement has a greater potential to encourage people to adopt healthy lifestyles. The main reason is that it is a positive and aspirational approach rather than <u>one</u> that deliberately targets <u>those</u> with fewer resources.

4 Career paths

Vocabulary

Dependent prepositions

1 Complete the sentences with a word from box A and a preposition from box B.

A
> conscious   desperate
> focus   invest   partner
> prevent   reliance

B
> for   from
> in   on (x2)
> of   with

1 Many universities now .... businesses so that students can get some practical experience before they graduate.

2 Some companies now have a heavy .... part-time staff to fill short-term vacancies.

3 I think it's a mistake for organisations not to .... their staff by providing high-quality training.

4 Our manager has asked us to .... planning for the next financial year.

5 In the UK, it is against the law to .... your employees .... taking sick leave.

6 However .... you may be .... a job, it is never a good idea to lie about your previous experience.

7 I would like to go into this in more depth but I'm .... the limited time we have left.

Adjective–noun collocations (1)

2 Complete the adjective that collocates with the noun in bold.

1 Carson & Co. has an excellent graduate training programme so there is f _ _ _ _ e **competition** to get a place on it.

2 In today's job market, you need s _ _ _ _ _ _ _ t **skills** to be sure of achieving job security.

3 Luke has v _ _ t **experience** in the field of mechanical engineering.

4 To succeed in publishing, you need to be able to work with a h _ _ h **degree** of accuracy.

5 Shannon has e _ _ _ _ _ _ e **knowledge** of intellectual property law.

6 Job satisfaction has a p _ _ _ _ _ _ l **impact** on a person's work ethic.

7 Our college has an u _ _ _ _ _ _ _ _ d **reputation** for supporting more gifted learners.

8 Young people nowadays are under c _ _ _ _ _ _ t **pressure** to succeed in their careers.

9 A l _ _ _ e **number** of 18-year-olds still don't know what they want to do in life.

10 There has been a c _ _ _ _ _ _ _ _ _ _ e **increase** in the number of students applying to study medicine.

3 For each of the sentences in Exercise 2, choose an adjective from the box which could replace the one you wrote. There may be more than one possible answer.

> excellent   expert   extensive   great   heavy
> high   huge   intense   large   vast

Grammar

Expressing possibility, probability and certainty

1 Circle the FOUR sentences that show the strongest possibility.

1 There is not much likelihood of my getting the promotion, but I'm going to apply for it anyway.

2 There is a small chance we'll get a pay rise this year.

3 James must have forgotten to lock the office door. He was the last one to leave.

4 The photocopier is bound to break down – it always does when I'm in a hurry.

5 Sarah just might agree to swap shifts with me.

6 It is highly likely there will be some kind of industrial action in the new year.

7 Luke is fairly likely to be made head of department when Lucy leaves.

8 Our working hours could well be increased next month.

2 Complete the sentences with an expression from the box.

> any chance   bound to   could have
> could well   every possibility
> more likely   possible   strong likelihood

1 There are three .... approaches to this task.

2 Is there .... you could work late this evening?

3 This .... be the most successful project we've ever completed.

4 Children are .... to learn if they are interested in the subject.

5 There's a .... that the workers will go on strike.

6 Julie .... been referring to Pete when she said that.

7 Simon is .... be sent on the course – he's the boss's favourite.

8 There's .... we'll have to make people redundant.

3 Find and correct the errors in these sentences. Two sentences are correct.

1 Serge is highly unlikely become a doctor.

2 Brooke mustn't have studied enough or she would have passed the exam.

3 We well could go out of business if things don't improve.

4 You might easy have mistaken George for his cousin – they look so alike.

5 Abigail is bound to coming top in the test – she's so smart.

6 Charlie can't have been running – he wasn't even out of breath.

7 One of the possible reason for rising unemployment is lack of consumer confidence.

8 The company could conceivably hire up to ten new members of staff.

Listening Part 3

Concentrate on the questions rather than the options. Note down your own answer before choosing the option that best matches your answer.

Exam advice

 5 **You will hear an interview with a man called Mike Jennings who works as a tea taster and a woman called Lara McDermott who imports tea to the UK. Choose the answer (A, B, C or D) which fits best according to what you hear.**

1 What does Mike say about how he got into tea tasting?
   A He was bored of the job he was doing.
   B He was persuaded by a friend to try it.
   C He unexpectedly discovered an interest in it.
   D His degree subject prepared him for it.

2 According to Mike, which factor is the most important for a tea taster?
   A experience of laboratory work
   B basic scientific knowledge
   C a good general education
   D natural sensitivity

3 What reason does Mike gives for tasters drinking their tea in a noisy way?
   A It is part of the traditional approach.
   B They are usually alone when tasting.
   C They drink from a spoon not a cup.
   D It helps them with their evaluation.

4 What does Lara say about top quality tea?
   A It is made using the 'cut, tear, curl' method.
   B Very little of it ends up in the UK.
   C Most of it is used to make teabags.
   D It tends to have a stronger flavour.

5 When asked about tea drinking habits in the UK, Lara explains that
   A young people are trying alternatives to black tea.
   B fewer people take milk and sugar in their tea.
   C older people are more likely to take sugar in tea.
   D most British people choose the same brands of tea.

6 When asked about the relative popularity of tea and coffee, what do Mike and Lara disagree about?
   A the primary cause of the increase in coffee drinking
   B the rate at which coffee drinking has increased
   C the main reason tea remains more popular than coffee
   D the way coffee is perceived by the British public

Reading and Use of English Part 8

You are going to read an article about the history and future of the working week in the UK. For questions 1–10, choose from the sections (A–D). The sections may be chosen more than once.

Which section

shows how to make employees work better at the start of the week?	1
explains the origins of long working hours in the UK?	2
reports research showing output is not increased by longer hours?	3
suggests some employees feel they are working too many hours?	4
gives an example of something that changed through workers taking time off?	5
mentions the beginnings of worker rights activism?	6
mentions potential alternatives to the 4-day week?	7
gives a reason for a national-level change to the working week?	8
outlines the benefits of the shorter working week?	9
describes the findings of an international body?	10

> **Exam advice**
>
> This part may consist of a continuous text, a text divided into sections or a series of short texts.
> The ideas in different parts of the text may appear similar so you will need to read the relevant parts in detail.

The working week in the UK

A

The five-day working week of Monday to Friday has been established for so long in the UK that we sometimes forget to question it. The status of Monday as the most dreaded day of the week is deeply embedded in UK culture. However, the working week hasn't always been this way, and employers and politicians are aware that the five-day week is far from universally accepted elsewhere. So, how did this current working pattern come about and why are so many people desperate to see it change?

The industrial revolution occurred in Britain in the 18th to early 19th centuries. Most work was seasonal and limited by daylight hours, and once factories had been built, their owners were reluctant to see their valuable machinery lying idle. This meant it was common for workers – even those under 18 – to do 14 to 16-hour days. The standard working week was six days as Sunday was dedicated to religious observance, meaning that workers had very little time for fun.

B

From the late 18th century, reformers began to agitate for more manageable working hours and, laws were passed in 1802 and 1819, limiting the working hours of children to 12 per day. It would be over a hundred years before working hours for women and children were fixed at nine per day. Adult men could still be forced to work unlimited hours. Eventually, the working week went down to five and a half days before it was lowered further to the current five-day week.

This working pattern was reflected in Europe and the United States where the industrial revolution continued. In 1926, the American car manufacturer Henry Ford was one of the first employers to give his workers a five-day working week, and the United States government introduced the five-day working week in 1932. This was implemented to counter unemployment caused by the Great Depression.

C

Those employers who adopted the five-day week, both in the UK and overseas, noticed their workers were invigorated on the first day of work, which led to a rise in productivity and reduced absenteeism. Employers and employees have naturally wondered if there are further gains to be made by knocking another day off the working week. It has now been almost a century since the five-day week was introduced, and many believe another change is long overdue.

Across the world, there have been numerous trials of the four-day week. Microsoft Japan tested it for a month and reported a 40% rise in productivity, not to mention a happier workforce. Research by the Organisation for Economic Cooperation and Development, a forum where the governments of 37 countries develop policies for sustainable economic growth, supports Microsoft's findings. The least productive countries were those with the highest number of working hours. Luxemburg, with an average working week of only 29 hours, was the most productive country studied. Yet, the 40-hour working week is still the norm.

D

So, what other alternatives are there to the 9 to 5 rat race? The compressed work week involves working three long (10+ hour days). While on the surface an attractive option, trials have found the longer hours on the working days negate the benefits of the extra free days. Various ways of working flexibly have been tried, and there are many organisations that have successfully implemented different types of arrangement.

In any case, employers and employees all understand the benefits of a happy workforce in economic and social terms and there are organisations that continue to campaign for the four-day week to become the standard. A survey conducted by the UK-based market research group, Yougov, reported that 60% of British workers still work more than they would like and 24% are overworking by at least ten hours per week. Although the data shows that fewer hours can lead to higher productivity, few employers have acted on it by reducing working hours. Campaigners believe that the 4-day week will only become a reality when the UK government enacts legislation to enforce it.

Writing Part 2
A letter

Exam advice

Follow letter-writing conventions, such as a salutation (e.g., Dear Sarah), explain your purpose for writing, use clear paragraphs and an appropriate ending.

1 Read the Part 2 task and say whether these sentences are True or False.

1 You have to write a letter to a close friend of yours.
2 You need information from the person you are writing to.
3 Your letter should be addressed to Anna.
4 Your letter should be formal in style.
5 You and Sarah work for the same company.

You have received a letter from an acquaintance.

> I don't know if you remember me, but we met at Manjit's party a few weeks ago. I've just got an interview with the company where you work. Could you give me some advice about how to prepare for it? What kind of questions do you think they might ask and what kind of research should I do beforehand? What should I wear to the interview?
>
> Maybe we could meet for lunch on the day? My shout!
>
> Thanks in advance for your help.
>
> Sarah

Write your **letter** in reply. You do not need to write postal addresses.

2 Complete the letter written by an exam candidate with a word or phrase from the box.

> collaboratively   position
> mission statement   organisational   policy
> team player   short-listed   workplace

Dear Sarah,

Thanks for your letter. Congratulations on getting an interview. I know lots of people applied for the **(1)** .... , so it's a real achievement to even get **(2)** ....

When I had an interview, I took part in a group task. We were asked to work **(3)** .... to solve a problem. What I learnt from the feedback they gave us was that they were less interested in the solution than in how we reached it. So, <u>the advice I'd give you</u> is invite others to contribute and react positively to their suggestions. <u>Try showing</u> you're confident, but also a **(4)** ....

In terms of research, I <u>suggest you finding</u> out what you can about the company. <u>You should go</u> through the website carefully and make notes on the **(5)** .... structure – who's in charge, what departments there are, and so on. You should also read the **(6)** .... That should give you an idea of the values and beliefs of the company. It also received an award recently for its environmental **(7)** .... , so <u>that's worth mention</u>!

Although it's quite an informal **(8)** .... with people often wearing jeans and a T-shirt, <u>I'd advice you to dress</u> formally for the interview. By 'formally', I mean a tailored skirt or trouser suit with a plain blouse. <u>Avoid to wear</u> too much make-up or jewellery.

I really hope this has helped. If you do want to get together, give me a call. Lunch sounds good!

All the best

Judith

3 The underlined phrases are used for giving advice. Are they used correctly? Correct any errors you find.

1 Try showing ....
2 the advice I'd give you ....
3 I suggest you finding ....
4 You should go ....
5 that's worth mention! ....
6 I'd advice you to dress ....
7 Avoid to wear ....

Vocabulary

Idiomatic language

1 Add a part of the body to complete the idiomatic expressions.

1 Some people pretend to be your friend but will stab you in the .... if they get the chance.

2 Jack is such a joker. He's always pulling my ....

3 Good luck with your interview today. I'll keep my .... crossed.

4 Our teacher sometimes turns a blind .... when students eat in class.

5 I was quite reluctant to come to the party, but Josh twisted my .... and here I am!

6 Megan isn't feeling well, so you all need to .... off and give her some space.

2 Complete the missing word in the idiomatic expression.

1 Ollie is a very argumentative boy – he's always trying to p _ _ _ fights with other children.

2 At break time, my job is to prevent students from j _ _ _ _ _ _ the lunch queue.

3 Sorry I couldn't take your call. I was t _ _ _ up in meetings all afternoon.

4 The robber got two years in prison, but considering how much he stole, I think he got off l _ _ _ _ _ _ .

5 My grandfather has been ill for a while but I think he's finally on the m _ _ _ .

6 I'd like to invite Jake to climb the mountain with me, but I'm not sure he's _ _ to it.

7 You get the tickets and I'll get the snacks. We can s _ _ _ _ _ up later.

8 You've been buying so many clothes lately, it's a w _ _ _ _ _ you can afford to pay your rent.

Grammar

Verbs followed by *to* + infinitive or the *-ing* form

1 Complete the extract from a blog post about weddings with the correct form of the verb in brackets.

When my boyfriend suggested **(1)** .... (get) married, I honestly intended **(2)** .... (stick) to an agreed budget for the wedding. Although lots of our friends had chosen **(3)** .... (have) destination weddings, in the Caribbean for example, we decided not to. We didn't want to risk **(4)** .... (leave) out friends and family who couldn't afford **(5)** .... (attend). I won't deny **(6)** .... (feel) slightly disappointed though, mainly because getting married in the UK always involves **(7)** .... (make) a plan B in case it rains. Anyway, the costs kept on **(8)** .... (grow). I had hoped **(9)** .... (keep) the guest list short, but it didn't work out that way. Apparently, I'd promised **(10)** .... (have) all eight of my little cousins as bridesmaids and pageboys!

2 Find and correct the errors in six of these sentences.

1 Would you mind to drop me off at the hospital on your way home?

2 Don't put off telling your parents you're engaged. It would be awful if they found out from someone else.

3 Annie pretended having a degree from a top university in order to get the job.

4 My exams are next week – I expect getting good grades in English and French but not in Maths.

5 Javier admitted be a little bit jealous of his brother's success.

6 I refuse apologising for telling the truth.

7 I always enjoy chatting to my cousin, Luke, at family events.

8 You're such a good speaker. Would you consider join the debating society?

9 Guests should avoid wearing either black or white to weddings in the UK.

10 We attempted to set up a charity event but it turned out to be too complicated.

Listening Part 1

6 You will hear three different extracts. For questions 1–6, choose the answer (A, B or C) which fits best according to what you hear. There are two questions for each extract.

Extract 1

You hear two friends talking about a holiday they went on in Norway.

1 The man and woman agree that
- **A** the scenery they saw was beautiful.
- **B** a railway they travelled on was impressive.
- **C** the railway was the best way to see the country.

2 What does the woman say about cycling around Norway?
- **A** She couldn't afford both bike hire and accommodation.
- **B** She would like to follow the same route as the train.
- **C** She'd rather cycle in a different area of the country.

Extract 2

You hear two friends talking about weddings.

3 Which aspect of their wedding plans do the woman and her fiancé disagree on?
- **A** the clothes they will both wear.
- **B** the food they will serve.
- **C** where the wedding will be held.

4 What surprised the man most about a wedding he attended?
- **A** The theme chosen by the bride and groom.
- **B** How much the couple spent on the wedding.
- **C** The number of guests the couple invited.

Extract 3

You hear a woman telling a friend about her scuba diving experience

5 Why was the woman reluctant to try scuba diving?
- **A** She thought that it was an unnatural activity.
- **B** She was concerned that it was something she couldn't afford.
- **C** She was scared that she'd encounter sea creatures.

6 How does the woman now feel about scuba diving?
- **A** It's a waste of money.
- **B** It's easier than expected.
- **C** It's a unique experience.

Reading and Use of English Part 4

Complete the second sentence so that it has a similar meaning to the first sentence, using the word given. Do not change the word given. You must use between three and six words, including the word given.

1 Richard didn't let anyone help him plan the party, but it was a great success.
INSISTENCE
The party was a great success
.... it by himself.

2 The prevention of further damage to the ancient monument is vital.
UTMOST
We must .... further damage to the ancient monument.

3 It is never possible to cancel bookings just before the event.
SHORT
Bookings cannot ....
under any circumstances.

4 Luisa did what she promised in spite of the difficulties she faced.
WORD
Luisa succeeded ....
although it was difficult for her.

5 None of the other comedians were anywhere near as funny as Max.
FAR
Max was ....
comedian in the show.

6 I worked all day and all night for the first time in my life.
CLOCK
I had .... before.

Reading and Use of English Part 7

You are going to read a magazine article about how the transition to adulthood is marked in different cultures. Six paragraphs have been removed from the article. Choose from the paragraphs A–G the one which fits each gap (1–6). There is one extra paragraph which you do not need to use.

What does it mean to 'come of age?' In legal or official terms, it means to reach the legal age of adulthood in the country where you live. However, different cultures around the world have always celebrated the transition from childhood to adulthood with important ceremonies and events which don't necessarily coincide with the individual becoming a legal adult. In the past, rites of passage could be challenging, painful or even dangerous.

1	

Fascinating though this is, in this article I want to reflect on what it means to come of age in an industrialised society in the 21st century by sharing the experience of young people I've spoken to. One thing I discovered was that even those who went through a coming-of-age ceremony rarely felt more grown up simply as a result of the event.

2	

Conversely, other young people consider themselves adults long before any celebration of the end of childhood. The reality of the modern world is that lots of children are deprived of a proper childhood due to circumstances beyond their control. The lack of an extended family to act as a support network can mean that adult responsibilities fall on young shoulders.

3	

Another common theme among the young people I spoke to was that it wasn't the day they turned 18 or 21 that made them an adult, but rather a major life event such as passing their driving test. 19-year-old Ben explained that in his village, children take the bus or get driven by their parents, whereas adults drive themselves.

4	

Moving out of home to live with other young people or into university accommodation was the definition of coming of age for many of those I spoke to. This of course didn't happen overnight but was a process of growing up over months or even years. Learning to cook, pay bills and budget was a learning curve that turned them from carefree teenagers to responsible adults.

5	

The fact that this amount of effort is involved is probably why most people said that, as much as they enjoyed parties and ceremonies to celebrate coming of age, they didn't really represent their personal transition to adulthood. The consensus was, moreover, that since everyone is unique, each person's journey towards being an adult will also be slightly different from anyone else's.

6	

What my conversations with these young people has highlighted is the disconnect between formal coming of age rituals and the lived experience of those participating in them, at least in modern, industrialised societies. In the future, perhaps we should focus less on formal ceremonies on fixed days and more on celebrating the achievements of young people as and when they occur.

A In addition to learning such practical domestic skills, the need to negotiate with others, reach agreement and manage conflict is a vital part of growing up. Many experience this as a key part of the messy process, requiring hard work and learning from one's mistakes, but resulting in maturity.

B Although leaving the family home like this is still an important rite of passage for many, celebrating it might stigmatise the many people who, for various reasons, have to move back in with their parents for a time after years of independence.

C This was certainly the experience of 18-year-old Shannon from Manchester, who has been a carer for her mother, Bridget, since she was just 10. 'My 18th birthday last month was a little strange because I'd been functioning as an adult for years,' she explained.

D Masai boys in Africa, for example, had to kill a male lion with just a spear. Similarly, boys of the Assyrian empire (1000–700 BC) had to undergo 15 years' hard training between the ages of five and 20 to be considered a man.

E 20-year-old Teresa from Texas, for instance, celebrated her 'quinceañera' at the age of 15 (quinceañera literally translates as 'the girl who is 15') but it was not until she left home to go to college when she was 19 that she actually made the transition to adulthood.

F This wide variety of paths to adult life has been explored through numerous films and books, showing how an individual's personality and circumstances lead to a range of experiences of what coming of age means.

G This varied according to location. For 21-year-old Londoner Todd, it wasn't so much how he got around that mattered, but getting a place of his own. Due to the high cost of housing, for Todd – as for most other young people – this meant sharing a flat.

Writing Part 2

A proposal

> A proposal is a mix of factual information and recommendations. Use persuasive language and a range of modal verbs to make suggestions and say what is possible.
>
> **Exam advice**

1 Read the proposal written by an exam candidate. Complete the gaps (1–8) by choosing the correct persuasive language phrases from the list below.

> a real need   provide an opportunity
> The principal objective   At present
> must take advantage of   Furthermore
> What's more   I propose

2 Match the underlined words in the text with their synonyms below.

1 image   ....
2 gives   ....
3 suitable   ....
4 mix   ....
5 official   ....
6 present   ....
7 report   ....
8 allows   ....

3 Now, think of a suitable heading for each paragraph.

Proposal for Greenborough University graduation ceremony

Greenborough University's first graduation ceremony will not only be for the new graduates, but it also provides a unique opportunity for the university to raise its profile among potential students. **(1)** .... of this proposal is to put forward ideas to make the most of this auspicious occasion.

(2) .... the university auditorium is not large enough to accommodate all the graduates and their families. I would therefore recommend the Festival Theatre. Its size and style make it a fitting venue for the occasion. **(3)** ...., its proximity to the university makes it easy for guests to move onto the campus for the remainder of the day.

After the formal proceedings, stalls could be set up on campus to sell university merchandise and provide food and drinks. A band could play live music. This will **(4)** .... for both students and parents to mingle and take photographs.

(5) ...., following consultation with residents at a recent town hall event, it was agreed that there is **(6)** .... for the university to be considered as a focal point of the area, which in turn enables the town to reap the benefits such an institution provides. Therefore, **(7)** .... that the graduation be streamed on social media, and that local media cover the event. This will give viewers the chance to see all that the university has to offer, and also showcases the area.

The first three years of Greenborough University have been a huge success. Now it **(8)** .... its first graduation ceremony to publicise the university's courses and attract new students.

6 Creative pursuits

Grammar

Avoiding repetition

1 Circle the correct alternative in *italics* to complete the sentences.

1 As soon as I heard about the new hybrid camera, I knew I had to get *one / it / this*.

2 A: Has Freya got tickets for the ballet tonight?
   B: Yes, I believe *such / so / yes*.

3 There are three new movies being released today, all of *them / which / those* I'm desperate to see.

4 I've told you to practise this piece every day and I hope you will do *it / this / so*.

5 I can't sing in tune but I really wish I *can / could / did*.

6 My daughter was chosen to play a solo in the school concert. *So / This / These* made the whole family proud.

7 Dylan was disappointed to miss the exhibition, but I assured him there would be *other / one / others*.

8 That actor has been in two movies and was excellent in *both / those / all*.

9 Marco lost his toy elephant but his dad bought him *one / another / it*.

10 Do you want any chips? Stay there, I'll get you *some / those / ones*.

2 Cross out the unnecessary words in these sentences.

1 Maddy would have been a ballerina if she had had the opportunity to be a ballet dancer.

2 My uncle promised to take me to the Liverpool game but he didn't take me to the Liverpool game.

3 I was sure we would win the match but the rest of the team weren't sure we would win the match.

4 There are no art galleries in my town but I wish there were some art galleries in my town.

5 I've never been to see an opera but I'd like to go and see an opera.

6 There was an amazing craft market in the square last Sunday and next Sunday there will be another amazing craft market in the square.

7 Noor isn't happy with her music classes but her brother is happy with his music classes.

8 Miss Nicholls asked Isaac to help clear up the mess but he refused to help clear up the mess.

3 Complete the blog post about living abroad with ONE suitable word in each gap. There may be more than one possible answer.

There are some things they say everyone should do in their lifetime. One of **(1)** .... is writing a book. **(2)** .... is living in a different country. I'm lucky enough to have done **(3)** .... of them. I'm not sure everyone could do the first **(4)** .... , but if you get the chance to do the second, I'd encourage you to do **(5)** .... You've probably read books about people **(6)** .... lives have been changed by the experience of extended travel, and it definitely changed **(7)** .... Many people who failed to take the opportunity to live abroad find, much later in life, that they wish they **(8)** .... **(9)** .... decide to travel after retirement and most of **(10)** .... have a wonderful experience.

Vocabulary

Adjective–noun collocations (2)

1 Choose the adjective in *italics* that best collocates with the noun in bold.

1 There has been a *fair / big* **amount** of interest in the idea of starting a drama club at school.

2 A *tremendous / high* **percentage** of students choose to take music or dance classes.

3 My hometown offers *a valuable / an endless* **range** of options for entertainment.

4 The one time I was in a play, I forgot my lines. It was a truly *terrible / tremendous* **experience**.

5 Our education system gives *high / huge* **importance** to creative subjects, which I feel is a good thing.

6 I started learning to play the piano in August and I think I've made *satisfactory / wide* **progress**.

7 Joanna's **experience** of working in radio will be *considerable / valuable* for her future career.

8 Universities look for students who have participated in a *limited / wide* **variety** of extra-curricular activities.

9 Sorry, I'm late. The **traffic** was really *heavy / high*.

10 A: What's that *terrible / heavy* **noise**?
B: It's my sister practising her violin.

2 Decide if the adjectives and nouns in bold collocate. If not, replace the adjective. Do NOT use the adjective used with the noun in Exercise 1.

1 The government only has a **limited amount** of money to spend on the arts.

2 Students can take lessons in a **high variety** of musical instruments.

3 Mila is making **strong progress** in her drama class.

4 We went on a walking tour of Edinburgh and it was an **amazing experience**.

5 Suddenly we heard a **tremendous noise** and ran for cover.

6 A **wide percentage** of the photographs were taken by children.

7 There was **big traffic** on our way to the theatre so we were almost late.

8 Most people don't realise the **tremendous importance** of introducing children to the arts.

9 Ayesha has gained **valuable experience** in the field of museum curation.

10 The shop has a **little range** of film and music posters.

Reading and Use of English Part 5

Questions in Part 5 may focus on paragraph, word or whole text level. Don't worry if you don't understand some of the words in a word-focused question – you will probably be able to work out the meaning by reading the surrounding sentences carefully.

Exam advice

You are going to read an article about ballet. Choose the answer (A, B, C or D) which you think fits best according to the text.

1 In the first paragraph, the writer expresses the opinion that

A Italian not French should be the language of ballet.

B King Louis had a negative impact on ballet's development.

C Noverre's influence has not received sufficient recognition.

D Catherine de Medici's role in ballet's development has been misrepresented.

2 In the second paragraph, which view is expressed about why modern ballets were initially disliked?

A The ballets didn't tell stories like classical ballets did.

B Classical techniques such as 'pointe' work were not included.

C People weren't ready for strong displays of emotion.

D People couldn't comprehend the role the music played.

3 In the third paragraph, what does the writer say about elitism in ballet in the UK?

A Ballet is more accessible than it is perceived to be.

B It is still very apparent in spite of industry attempts to combat it.

C It will only change when the cost of going to performances reduces.

D Efforts to widen access to ballet have made a real difference.

4 In the fourth paragraph, the writer shows surprise at the fact that

A female dancers are expected to appear so light.

B writers continue to create stereotypical roles.

C more boys are not interested in doing ballet.

D there are not many women in management roles.

5 Why does the writer use the phrase 'in thrall' in line 23?

A to emphasise the strong influence ballet has on audiences.

B to suggest audiences find ballet difficult to understand.

C to imply the strength and stamina of dancers is an illusion.

D to remind readers of the royal origins of the dance form.

6 What does the writer suggest about the future of ballet in the final paragraph?

A It is up to governments to ensure its future success.

B There is a chance the dance form might not survive.

C The major ballet companies are not committed to change.

D Ballet lovers should do more for the wider community.

The history and future of ballet

As a young child learning ballet, I was bemused by the language the teacher used: *plié, pas de chat, jeté*. Having been told the words were French, I assumed, wrongly as it turned out, that France was the country of origin of the dance form. In fact, it first emerged at the Italian royal court in the 15th century; it was Catherine de Medici, married to the French monarch, who financially supported the art form in the French court, beginning an association that lasts to the present day. A century after its introduction to the aristocracy of France, another of their number, Louis XIV the 'sun king', standardised and popularised ballet. As a dancer himself, he raised its status from enjoyable pastime to profession. Nevertheless, unlike many commentators, I would give more credit for the development of ballet as we know it now to balletmaster Jean Georges Noverre, who began using the dance form to relate popular tales.

As with other art forms, Romanticism started to heavily shape the development of ballet in the 19th century. This movement concerned itself with the supernatural world of spirits and magic, and ballerinas were portrayed as passive and fragile. Around this time, another superpower of the dance form – Russia – entered the stage, producing some of the greatest classical ballets of all time, such as Swan Lake and The Nutcracker. The purpose was to display classical techniques, including pointe work (ballerinas on

tiptoe) and high extensions. In my view, it was not so much the lack of plot or the intense focus on human emotion that made modern ballets unpopular with audiences when they were first introduced in the early 20th century. They were probably more offended by the inharmonious music, whose meaning and purpose they are likely to have misunderstood.

Throughout its history, ballet has been accused of elitism, which in my experience here in the UK is fully justified. In Britain, it is generally the preserve of the wealthy or middle classes, and it is unlikely that a working-class individual will take it up as a career. This is partly a result of the perception of ballet as being part of an inaccessible world – hardly surprising given its origins in the royal courts. While many UK ballet schools and companies have tried hard to diversify by offering scholarships to less affluent but talented dancers, the reality is that this is insufficient to attract any but the most determined. The chances of working-class youngsters even being exposed to ballet are low, since live performances are prohibitively expensive and little coverage is given to the art form on TV. Since most ballet dancers begin their training at a young age, what I've noticed is that it is those whose parents are aware of the dance form and have a high income who have access to classes.

Like so many spheres of human activity, ballet has inherited a legacy of sexism. As anyone who

has attended a ballet class will attest, females greatly outnumber males and in classical ballet at least, gender roles are fixed. Two mainstays of ballet – lifting and pointe work – emphasise the strength of the male and the female's need for support. Dancing on tiptoe makes the woman look delicate and weightless. I've always wondered why so few boys take ballet classes; after all, they appear strong and protective on stage. If anything, it is the women I would expect to be discouraged by the passive role allotted to them. Conversely, senior management within the world of ballet is overwhelmingly male; sadly, only a few women have managed to break through the glass ceiling and become creative directors of ballet companies.

The talent, strength and stamina of dancers have held crowds **in thrall** Line 23 for centuries, and to this day, ballet continues to fascinate and inspire. Its regal beginnings and romantic associations set it apart from other types of dance; yet those involved in ballet, here in the UK at least, still have work to do to make the art form accessible to all, or its very existence may be threatened. It would be unrealistic to suggest governments should fund initiatives to widen participation in the arts while other more basic needs are left unmet. Instead, those who love ballet could be more proactive in enabling anyone with an interest to get involved either as dancers or supporters. Taking such steps could help secure the future of this beautiful art form.

Listening Part 2

7 **You will hear a university lecturer called Jenny Warren giving a talk about culture. Complete the sentences with a word or short phrase.**

1 Jenny gives some examples of fruits that don't grow in .... due to the prevailing conditions.

2 Jenny says that fast cooking techniques are used in regions where the availability of .... is limited.

3 Jenny feels that comparing culture to an .... helps people to understand what culture is.

4 Jenny likes the example of .... as a cultural behaviour that isn't easy to pick up on.

5 In the popular model of culture that Jenny gives, she says that accepted behaviour and beliefs are represented by the .... of the tree.

6 In Jűrgen Bolton's model of culture, ... are represented by the bottom of the sand dune.

7 Jenny gives an example of a traditional style of ...., as an expression of cultural identity by a particular group.

8 Jenny gives the example of .... as a language which has gained more speakers after a period of decline.

Writing Part 2

A review

Look at the following Writing Part 2 (Review) task.

REALITY TV REVIEWS WANTED

Send us a review of a reality TV show you've watched. Tell us what you think of the concept of the show and about the highs (or lows) of a season you've watched – or rewatched – recently.

Who is your favourite character and why?
Write your review in 220–260 words.

---

1 **Complete the collocations with a word from below.**

> reality plan basket end
> recipe home bunch household

Great British Bake Off (GBBO) is surprisingly addictive. Every season a group of amateur bakers from all over Britain compete to be crowned Britain's best baker. Why I like it is that, unlike other **(1)** .... shows, the aim is not to achieve either fame or fortune. The prize is just a cake stand and a **(2)** .... of flowers, but people are proud to take part and do it for the experience.

There have been about 10 or 11 seasons of GBBO and I've been glued to it from the very first. The contestants are really relatable – you feel like they could be your co-workers or neighbours so you find yourself rooting for them.

For me, the highlight of the season I've just watched was a challenge where they had to make a picnic **(3)** .... and fill it with food, but it was all made from cakes and biscuits. The **(4)** .... results were stunning: so imaginative and technically brilliant. It is always disappointing, though, when things don't go to **(5)** .... One man made an ice-cream cake on a scorching summer's day; it melted, and he threw it in the bin.

There are so many characters associated with GBBO. The judges and presenters are all **(6)** .... names. My absolute favourite is one of the winners who did go on to be famous, Nadiya Hussain. She was just a typical **(7)** .... baker but since winning, has gone on to publish **(8)** .... books and become a TV presenter herself.

Whether you're into baking or not, I highly recommend GBBO for its creativity and excitement.

2 **Read the review by an exam candidate. Which adjectives has the writer used to describe the following?**

1 GBBO ....
2 The contestants ....
3 The picnic baskets ....
4 When things don't go to plan ....
5 The summer's day. ....
6 Nadiya Hussain ....

3 **Find the expressions the writer uses:**

1 to introduce her opinion (paragraph 1)
2 to say she hasn't been able to stop watching it (paragraph 2)
3 to say you feel like supporting the contestants (paragraph 2)
4 to give her opinion of the best part of the series (paragraph 3)
5 to say which contestant she preferred (paragraph 4)
6 to advise others to watch the show (paragraph 5)

7 In your free time

Vocabulary

Complex prepositions

1 Complete the sentences with a word from box A and a preposition from box B. You can use the words in box B more than once.

A

> account   behalf   aid   exchange   far
> keeping   means   place   regard

B

> for   from   of   to   with

1 On .... the entire cast, I'd like to welcome you to tonight's performance.
2 That new building is just not in .... the rest of the architecture in the area.
3 The school children have been making and selling Christmas cards in .... the homeless shelter.
4 Sophie gets to ride the horses three times a week in .... cleaning out the stables.
5 In .... our usual warm-up band, we are pleased to welcome The Moonlighters!
6 The skating club is closing down on .... the costs involved in running it.
7 This is not the first time Rupert has sung a solo – .... it, in fact.
8 Skiers are transported to the top of the mountain by .... a pulley system known as a 'button lift'.
9 I'm calling with .... the mountain bike you advertised on the Cycle World website.

Money words

2 Complete the missing letters in the money-related phrases.

1 Golf is my favourite sport, but unfortunately, it c _ _ _ _ _ a f _ _ _ _ _ _ to join a club.
2 A: Can I p _ _ b _ c _ _ _ _ ?
  B: No, I'm sorry. It's cash only.
3 I feel guilty that my parents had to t _ _ _ o _ _ a l _ _ _ _ to pay my university fees.
4 Alberto didn't get the job. I think he is just too modest to s _ _ _ _ h _ _ _ _ _ _ _ the way you need to in an interview.
5 It's possible to e _ _ _ _ a l _ _ _ _ _ _ by collecting and selling things other people have thrown away.
6 When I was a student, I used to m _ _ _ _ a quick b _ _ _ _ by playing my saxophone at the underground station.
7 In the summer, we're going to r _ _ _ _ a house in the mountains and h _ _ _ _ a car to get us there.
8 I'll l _ _ _ _ you the money as long as you promise to p _ _ it b _ _ _ _ .
9 Look how enormous that house is. The people that live there must have m _ _ _ _ _ to b _ _ _ _ .
10 I think it's sad to see people who can't a _ _ _ _ _ _ their medical treatment trying to r _ _ _ _ money online to pay for it.

Money idioms

3 Match the money idioms with their meaning.

1 money doesn't grow on trees ....
2 paid peanuts ....
3 hold the purse strings ....
4 pay through the nose ....
5 put your money where your mouth is ....
6 spend money like water ....
7 rolling in money ....
8 pay my own way ....
9 break the bank ....

a not rely on others financially
b have to pay too much for something
c very wealthy
d get a very low salary
e be more than you can afford to pay
f be careful with money as it is limited
g do something positive instead of just talking
h be in control of the money
i be wasteful with your money

4 Complete the sentences with an idiom from Exercise 3 in the correct form.

Example: Don't worry, it's only a few coffees. It won't *break the bank.*

1 When I started the job, I was
...., but it didn't
bother me because I was gaining valuable experience.

2 Billy is .... at the
moment. First a new motorbike, then all those new clothes
and now he's bought himself a guitar.

3 I'd like to buy some new software but it's the head of
department who ....
and I'm not sure she'll agree.

4 Buying theatre tickets through an agent can mean you
.... – it can be
cheaper to buy direct from the box office.

5 Have you seen the house Salman's parents live in?
It's massive! They must be
....

6 No, you can't have a new Xbox.
...., you know!

7 It's easy to go on about what should be done to help the
poor. Instead, why don't you
.... ?

8 It was very kind of Jeff to offer to pay for the
whole holiday, but personally, I like to
....

Grammar

Linking ideas: relative and participle clauses

1 Complete the sentences with a relative pronoun in each gap. If the pronoun is optional, put brackets around it. Add commas to the sentence if needed.

1 The TV channel .... people watch most is the one with no advertisements.
2 The man .... café went out of business last year has opened a new one.
3 *Mean Girls* .... was released in 2004 was a typical American high school movie.
4 *Mr Bean* was a TV show .... was loved by adults and children alike.
5 The youth club .... my parents met in the 1990s is still popular today.
6 My elder brother .... was always fixing things around the house has just qualified as an engineer.
7 Have you ever met anyone .... has a black belt in karate?
8 Parkour .... is similar to free running can be quite dangerous.
9 The trainers .... I wanted are too expensive.
10 Harlan Coben .... books I love is an American novelist.

2 Join the two sentences using a participle clause.

Example:
I'm a fitness fanatic. I go to the gym every day.
Being *a fitness fanatic, I go to the gym every day.*

1 Josefina ran down the road. She was calling her brother's name.
Josefina ....
2 This house was built in 1595. It is the oldest house in the village.
Built ....
3 Evie studied French at university. She was able to understand the film.
Having ....
4 This lace is really beautiful. It was made by hand.
Made ....
5 The director made a speech. He thanked everyone for their help.
The director ....
6 Alvin passed grade 6 piano. He moved to the grade 7 class.
Having ....
7 Coffee is good for you. You should drink it in small quantities.
Drunk ....
8 Maurice handed me the money. He looked at me suspiciously.
Looking ....

Linking ideas: apposition

3 Cross out any unnecessary words in these sentences.

1 Turn right at the Beacon Centre, which is the building next to the school.
2 Jessica, who is the girl I told you about, is standing over there.
3 Freedom, which is the greatest gift of all, is often taken for granted.
4 The O'Connor twins, who are well-known ice-skaters, used to live next door to us.
5 Rounders, which is a baseball-like sport, is very popular in England.
6 My students, who were all Japanese, were amazing at origami.

Reading and Use of English Part 1

Read the text below and decide which answer (A, B, C or D) best fits each gap. There is an example at the beginning (0).

Example:

0 **A** head **B** mind **C** brain **D** thought

Mini golf goes hi-tech

When someone mentions mini-golf, what comes to **(0)** ....*B*....... ? For many older British people, it is associated with seaside holiday resorts of their childhood. Well, mini-golf has undergone a **(1)** .... over the last few years, and Puttshack's new venues are a far **(2)** .... from the cheap and cheerful mini-golf courses of the past.

Puttshack offers a hi-tech gaming experience suitable for the 21st century. The electronic scoring system ensures that you will never **(3)** .... count of the score. Sensors record every shot you take, an approach that **(4)** .... that cheating is impossible, meaning that you never need to **(5)** .... a blind eye to your friend's extra stroke.

Mini-golf is a fun night out which **(6)** .... a balance between skill and fun. And even if you've never had a **(7)** .... desire to play a traditional round, Puttshack's fun but affordable experience makes it somewhere even complete novices can really **(8)** .... into the great game of mini-golf.

1	**A** transfer	**B** conversion	**C** transformation	**D** shift
2	**A** cry	**B** shout	**C** yell	**D** call
3	**A** drop	**B** lose	**C** miss	**D** forget
4	**A** confirms	**B** ensures	**C** establishes	**D** maintains
5	**A** look	**B** have	**C** give	**D** turn
6	**A** forces	**B** hits	**C** strikes	**D** makes
7	**A** burning	**B** scorching	**C** glowing	**D** heated
8	**A** go	**B** catch	**C** fall	**D** get

Listening Part 4

8 You will hear five short extracts in which people are talking about taking part in different events for charity.

TASK ONE
Choose from the list (A-H) the main reason each speaker gives for taking part in the event.

A to show appreciation for some help
B to raise money for specific equipment
C to encourage others to fundraise
D to overcome a fear
E to celebrate the life of a loved one
F to raise awareness of an issue
G to make a friend proud
H to fulfil a personal ambition

TASK TWO
Choose from the list (A-H) the way the speaker feels about their event now.

A proud of their achievement
B disappointed it didn't go well
C excited about a further similar exploit
D worried about the consequences
E relieved that they survived
F sad about others' reactions
G happy about an unexpected outcome
H frustrated by delays

Speaker 1		**1**	Speaker 1		**6**
Speaker 2		**2**	Speaker 2		**7**
Speaker 3		**3**	Speaker 3		**8**
Speaker 4		**4**	Speaker 4		**9**
Speaker 5		**5**	Speaker 5		**10**

Writing Part 2

A letter

Read the Writing Part 2 exam question and the model answer.

> **Exam advice**
>
> Even if you are writing an informal letter, using topic sentences in each paragraph helps your reader to follow your writing, and helps you remember to include all the points you need to cover in your answer.

> You receive a letter from a friend.
>
> Part of my company is moving to another town and has asked me to relocate. However, I don't know what to do. How will I meet people and find somewhere to live? I may also miss my old colleagues. Maybe moving isn't such a good idea.
>
> Natasha
>
> Write to your friend giving your opinion and offering advice.

1 A student has written a response to the above exam task. Put the paragraphs into the correct order.

A Secondly, I doubt finding accommodation will be a huge issue, either. **(1)** *How about/Why don't you* find out if there's anyone you could share a flat with? If not, most estate agents arrange house shares for young people, which could also be a way to make new friends. You **(2)** *may/could* also ask your HR department if they're able to help.

B Since you're not leaving your company, I'm sure there will be plenty of opportunities to meet up with the colleagues you work with now. They might even get the chance to relocate later on as your boss might decide to move more employees once the new branch is settled there. In any case, you definitely **(3)** *couldn't/shouldn't* let this hold you back.

C It was great to hear from you. How exciting to get the opportunity to move to another town! That's amazing!

D So, all in all, it sounds like a marvellous chance to expand your horizons. Starting a new venture together is sure to be a bonding experience and should be good for your CV too. **(4)** *If I were you/ If I'm you*, I'd definitely give it a go.

E It's natural to have a few concerns about such a big chance but in my opinion, there's no need to worry too much about it. First, I assume lots of your colleagues will be going too so I don't think meeting people will be a problem. Everyone will be in the same boat, so at least at first, you can all do stuff together in the evenings. **(5)** *I'll/I'd* advise you to join a gym as you'll meet plenty of like-minded people there.

2 The writer has used several phrases to give advice to her friend. Choose the correct option in the phrases in *italics*.

3 Find a word or phrase in the letter which means:

1 big problem (para A)
2 arrangements where people who don't know each other live together (para A)
3 prevent you from doing something (para B)
4 have more and different experiences (para D)
5 something which brings people close together (para D)
6 try something (para D)
7 be in a similar position to others (para E)
8 those with similar ideas to you (para E)

Grammar

Reported speech

1 Rewrite the underlined parts of the conversation in reported speech.

1 S: So, <u>what did you study at university</u>, Jim
Sonia asked Jim what he'd studied at university.

2 J: <u>I didn't go to university at all</u>. I did an apprenticeship.

3 S: Oh, that's interesting. <u>That's what I'm thinking of doing</u>.

4 J: Well, <u>I'd highly recommend it</u>.

5 S: Yes, that way, <u>I'll start earning money straight away</u>.

6 J: <u>Have you considered the possibility of an apprenticeship here?</u>

7 S: Oh, that would be great. <u>Do you know when the closing date for applications is</u>?

8 J: Let me check. <u>It's next Friday</u>. That should give you enough time. I'll help you if you want.

9 S: <u>I've been hoping you'd say that</u>! Thank you so much!

2 Find and correct the errors in seven of the reported sentences. One has been done for you. Tick the two correct sentences.

1 'I only listen to the radio in the car.'
Hannah said she has only listened to the radio in the car.
Hannah said she only listened to the radio in the car.

2 'How long have you been living here?'
Becky asked Arturo how long he has been living here.

3 'I didn't enjoy the film because I'd seen it before.'
Charlotte told me that she didn't enjoy the film because she saw it before.

4 'Have you ever appeared on TV?'
Charlie wanted to know whether have I ever appeared on TV.

5 'I'll read the report tomorrow.'
Carmen said that she would read the report the following day.

6 'I'm still waiting to hear if I got the job at the newspaper.'
Tim told me that I was still waiting to hear if I got the job at the newspaper.

7 'My mum didn't watch the news yesterday.'
Connie said that her mum hasn't watched the news yesterday.

8 'I won't be working next Saturday.'
Iago told me that he wouldn't be working the following Saturday.

9 'Why are you staring at me?'
David asked me why was I staring at him?

Transitive verbs

3 Find and correct the errors in seven of these sentences. One has been done for you. Tick the four correct sentences.

1 I wasn't really interested in the concert, but my friends persuaded to go.
*I wasn't really interested in the concert, but my friends persuaded **me** to go.*

2 My school arranged me to do work experience at an advertising agency.

3 The law requires to wear a seatbelt, even in the back seat.

4 Luckily, my best friend reminded to me to give in my assignment before the deadline.

5 My dad was really happy that you mentioned him in your speech at the wedding.

6 The police officer instructed Ricardo to get out of the car.

7 You should admit your parents what you did.

8 The lifeguard warned us not to dive off the rocks.

9 I'm glad you allowed me to go to the party – I had a blast.

10 Our teacher has just informed about the test next week.

11 Amalie refused me to help with the project.

Vocabulary

Talking verbs

1 Complete the sentences with the correct form of a verb from box A and a word or phrase from box B. You can use some verbs more than once. Use the words and phrases in box B once only.

A

> comment   discuss   express   mention
> say   speak   talk   tell

B

> anyone   clearly   her mind   my name   my thanks
> nonsense   nothing   on the fact
> the questions   the truth   ~~to my friends~~

1   I ___'ll talk to my friends___ to see if any of them can help you.
2   Please don't ....! It's a secret.
3   I'd like you to .... in groups of four or five.
4   When you give your presentation, remember to .... so the people at the back can hear.
5   The shop is owned by my uncle. If you ...., they'll give you a discount.
6   Stop ....! There's no such thing as aliens.
7   I know I lied before, but I promise I .... now.
8   Tania is a girl who always ...., even if what she has to say is unpopular.
9   If they ask you where you were that night, ... Just keep quiet.
10   I'm writing to .... for the beautiful gift you sent for our wedding.
11   Jacob was interviewed by a journalist, but he refused .... that he had been there when the crime was committed.

Prefixes and suffixes

2 Add the correct prefix.

1   Joanne was quite ....popular in school. She didn't have a lot of friends.
2   I started a new job last week. I seem to be more ....experienced than everyone else. They've been doing the job for years.
3   In Singapore, it is ....legal to chew gum.
4   The director was ....satisfied with the negative reviews of his latest film.
5   A person's family connections are ....relevant to whether they can do the job.
6   The editor is ....certain about whether your article will be included in this week's magazine.
7   It doesn't matter if your English is ....perfect as long as it can be understood.
8   The company changed their supplier because the previous one was ....efficient.

3 Add a prefix from the box to a word in each sentence. Use one prefix twice.

> re   under   inter   dis   mis

1   I approve of the way some newspapers exaggerate the truth.
2   We're going to buy some more food as we estimated how many people would come to the party.
3   Our local council has decided to construct the library building, which was partially destroyed by fire.
4   Ella didn't do well in her assignment because she completely understood the instructions.
5   The organisation I work for is planning to locate to a city where rents are cheaper.
6   Julian would do well in a role which involves acting with the public.

4 Add a prefix to the word in bold to create a more logical sentence. Make any other necessary changes.

1   My neighbours are all complaining about the **efficient** of the local council.   *inefficiency*
2   I'm afraid there seems to have been an **understand**. I didn't post that picture.
3   The police are going to organise a **construct** of the crime as a way of appealing for witnesses.
4   It's **legal** to tap people's phones but some journalists will do it if they get the chance.
5   Sam is too **experience** to handle a case without supervision.
6   I don't like reading novels. I prefer **fiction**, especially books about nature.

5 Complete the sentences using a word from the box. Add a prefix and/or suffix where necessary and make any other changes needed.

> legal   relevant   approve
> perfect   pilot   popular   satisfy

1   Most children are desperate for the .... of their peers.
2   Despite a few minor ...., this is one of the best diamonds I've ever seen.
3   I fail to see the .... of your argument to the current situation.
4   The students expressed their .... with the food in the school canteen.
5   Oakfield High School was shut down due to its .... with local families.
6   Captain Saunders passed control to his .... for the final descent into Frankfurt.
7   He was sent to prison once the .... of his actions was established.

Reading and Use of English Part 3

Read the text below. Use the word given in capitals at the end of some of the lines to form a word that fits in the gap in the same line. There is an example at the beginning (0).

Remember some words might need to be made negative, so check the meaning of each sentence carefully. In some cases, you might need to add both a prefix and a suffix.

Exam advice

Example (0): INVENTOR

The origins of printing in the modern age

The German **(0)** INVENTOR, Johannes Gutenberg, is widely credited with introducing the printing press to Europe. A basic press had been used in China from the 9th century but Gutenberg's **(1)** .... adaptation of the press in around 1450 is said to have ushered in the modern age. — **INVENT** / **INNOVATE**

Perhaps Gutenberg's greatest **(2)** .... was his first print run: 300 copies of the Bible in Latin, which took him three years to complete. Despite having the **(3)** .... to produce printed materials, the lack of people able to read meant **(4)** .... of the books was a challenge. However, printing did change the **(5)** .... of news as it became normal to get daily updates by listening to a paid reader. — **ACCOMPLISH** / **CAPABLE** / **DISTRIBUTE** / **CONSUME**

It is **(6)** .... that the printing press helped spread scientific ideas. A barrier to progress before the printing press was that, by copying by hand, a lot of data was **(7)** .... noted down. Printing solved this issue, as it allowed the exact replication of pages again and again. — **DENY** / **ACCURATE**

Although he died penniless, Gutenberg is considered one of the most **(8)** .... people in history. — **INFLUENCE**

Listening Part 3

9 You will hear an interview in which two foreign correspondents called Mark Shelby and Carol Bentall are talking about their work. Choose the answer (A, B, C or D) which fits best according to what you hear.

You might not get all the answers on the first listening: instead, cross off any answers you are sure are not correct so that you have fewer options to choose from on the second listening. *Exam advice*

1 What does Mark feel is the most important quality in a foreign correspondent?
   A a desire to understand a situation in depth
   B a natural talent for writing news stories
   C a skill in identifying what others miss
   D a single-minded approach to getting a story

2 When asked about the most challenging part of the job, Mark suggests that he
   A finds the interpersonal aspects difficult.
   B would prefer more comfortable accommodation.
   C would like more time with his loved ones.
   D often worries about his personal safety.

3 How does Carol feel about the role of technology in her work?
   A She feels pressure to gain technical skills.
   B She worries unnecessarily about technical problems.
   C She gets frustrated by delays in getting through.
   D She misses certain aspects of older technology.

4 What is Mark's opinion on how the internet has affected his work?
   A It is more difficult to find reliable sources.
   B It has made reporting on global disputes more complex.
   C It has meant that fewer people refuse to talk to him.
   D It has become harder to hide his own views.

5 How does Carol feel about the memorable incident she describes?
   A angry that she had been misled
   B accepting of the situation
   C jealous of the other reporters
   D embarrassed about her mistake

6 Mark and Carol agree that young people wanting to be foreign correspondents should
   A do their best to prioritise ethical behaviour.
   B become fluent in at least one other language.
   C avoid worrying about the risks involved.
   D focus on building a name for themselves.

Writing Part 2
A proposal

> **Exam advice**
> Use a range of modal verbs such as *should*, *would*, *could* and *will* to make suggestions and explain the potential results of your proposal.

1 Answer True (T) or False (F).

1 A proposal will always be written for someone in authority.
2 You should make as many suggestions as possible.
3 You are expected to give reasons for your recommendations.
4 You should use persuasive language.
5 You shouldn't organise your proposal into headed sections.
6 The language of a proposal tends to be quite formal.

> You work for Webster's, an international company which sells clothing aimed at the young adult market. The manager believes the current website doesn't do enough to encourage customers to look at the products and has asked staff to give their opinion on how to change the website. You decide to write a proposal, suggesting how the website can be improved, outlining what extra features should be included on the website and explaining how this would make the website more attractive for customers and lead to increased sales.
>
> Write your **proposal**.

2 Read the proposal written by a student as a response to the above task. Does the proposal:

1 explain why the website doesn't do enough to encourage customers to look at the products?
2 explain how the website could be improved?
3 outline some extra features and say how they would make the website more attractive for customers?

3 Put the adjectives in *italics* into the correct column.

Positive	Negative
state-of-the-art	

4 Which modal/auxiliary verbs does the writer use for the following functions?

1 To say something that is going to happen (Paragraph 1)
2 To say something is necessary (Paragraph 3)
3 To refer to an imagined case (Paragraphs 3 and 4)
4 To say what is the ideal thing to do (Paragraph 4)
5 To express present possibility (Paragraph 4)
6 To express future possibility (Paragraph 5)

Introduction

The current website was set up by a firm of IT designers in 2016. While it was *state-of-the-art* at the time, it is now looking *dated* and *amateur*. Webster's now has the in-house expertise to create our own site, which reflects our values and priorities. In this proposal, I will outline my vision for our website.

Aesthetics

For many of our customers, the website is the first point of contact with the company; it is therefore vital to have a *superior* site, which gives an *exceptional* first impression. The current site is too *cluttered* and uses *drab* colours. I propose giving it a cleaner, more *minimalist* look and introducing bright, fresh colours, such as orange, yellow and green.

Functionality

Feedback from our customers suggests the website needs to be more *user-friendly*. A common complaint was that locating products was *time-consuming*. I recommend a menu with fewer options with buttons on the landing page for the most popular pages. In addition, it would help customers if we displayed our contact information more prominently.

New features

Being part of a *saturated* market, we should raise our site above the average. I suggest including styling tips to show how our clothes can be used to create a *distinctive* look. Similarly, an *interactive* feature demonstrating which styles suit which body type would be a highly *innovative* way to attract customers and sell more clothes.

Conclusion

I recommend the establishment of a committee to share ideas for the upgrade of the website and decide on how the changes could be implemented.

9 Invention and innovation

Grammar

Future perfect and continuous, *be* + *to* infinitive

1 Complete the sentences with the correct form of the verb in brackets. Use future perfect (simple or continuous), future continuous or *be* + *to* infinitive.

1 We've just heard that the company .... by an American tech firm. (take over)

2 New laptops .... to all employees by the end of the month. (issue)

3 Do you think we .... all .... electric cars as early as 2030? (drive)

4 The prime minister .... the nation at 5 pm today. (address)

5 Do you think your husband .... us for dinner? (join)

6 By the time we get there we .... for almost 24 hours. (travel)

7 I expect we .... all night to get this order finished. (work)

8 There .... a debate in parliament tomorrow about 5G technology. (be)

9 This time next week Jo and Tom .... Mount Everest. I hope they make it to the top. (climb)

Verb patterns – objects, reflexives and reciprocals

2 Find and correct the errors in seven of these sentences. The first one has been done for you.

1 My dad taught (to swim me) when I was five years old.
   me to swim

2 My cousin and I never really liked each another, but we get on OK nowadays.

3 Evelyn decided to treat herself to a new tablet.

4 I'm going to knit for my sister's new baby a jumper.

5 Anouk frequently sends text messages her colleagues.

6 My neighbour and I help one other when we can.

7 I borrowed money from my uncle to buy a new phone.

8 John walked along the office corridor muttering to hisself.

9 I think you owe to me an explanation for borrowing my car without asking.

Vocabulary

Technology collocations

1 Choose the word that best collocates with the noun in bold.

1 I think people should *exercise* / *make* more of an **effort** to recycle packaging.

2 If we keep going on about the issue of online safety, there is a danger that teenagers will *lose* / *take* **interest**.

3 I took some painkillers but they haven't *made* / *taken* **effect** yet.

4 You can sit and *dream up* / *come up* **ideas** all day long but unless you act on them, nothing will change.

5 Due to social media, society has *made* / *undergone* a dramatic **transformation** in the last 15 years.

6 The decision to close one of the runways at our local airport has *taken* / *made* an **impact** on the surrounding area.

7 I suggest you *exercise* / *take* **caution** when shopping online – not all sites are trustworthy.

Multi-word verbs

2 Complete the sentences with the correct form of a verb from A and a preposition from B.

A
| hack   lock |
| pop   run   scroll |
| shut   sign |

B
| down   in |
| into   out (x2) |
| through   up |

1 I've forgotten my password so it didn't let me ....

2 Sara's been using her phone more than usual this month and she's already .... of data.

3 I get so many work emails that it takes ages to .... them and find the one I need.

4 Oh no! I've been .... of my account because I entered the wrong password three times.

5 Adverts for virus guards keep .... on my screen. It's so annoying!

6 People who manage to .... government computer systems should be offered jobs, not sent to prison.

7 If you forget to .... your computer, you won't get software updates.

action, activity, event and programme

3 Match the two halves of the sentences.

1 The management have finally decided to take decisive
2 My neighbour is angry that I park in front of his house and now he has threatened
3 There is a new programme in our area
4 I wouldn't have anything to wear to a glamorous
5 The police are concerned that there has been no activity
6 My son doesn't like sport – he prefers indoor
7 Unfortunately, the photocopier is out of
8 There are never any interesting programmes
9 Children find learning about historical

a activities such as playing board games.
b action at the moment.
c events more exciting if they can visit the sites where they took place.
d action against the strikers.
e to help older people develop computer skills.
f on TV on a Saturday night.
g on his bank account since he went missing.
h me with legal action.
i event like a ball.

4 Circle the correct alternative in *italics* to complete the sentences.

1 In my opinion, the *action / event* was a great success.
2 Last October, the theatre put on an excellent *event / programme* of Shakespeare's plays.
3 Children often like songs where they can do the *actions / activities*.
4 What kind of *actions / activities* do you enjoy doing in your free time?
5 The next *event / programme* will be a basketball tournament.
6 We can advise you on which *programme / activity* of study would suit you best.
7 OK class, we are now going to move on to the next *programme / activity*. Please get into groups.
8 We arrived at the sports field early, well rested and ready for *action / activity*.

Listening Part 1

Read both questions carefully before the extract begins as there won't be a pause before the section of text that provides the answer to the second question.

Exam advice

 You will hear three different extracts. Choose the answer (A, B or C) which fits best according to what you hear. There are two questions for each extract.

Extract 1
You hear two students talking about building a drone.
1 According to the girl, what does their project demonstrate?
  A the efficiency of the drone they are building
  B the effect on direction caused by the propellers
  C the relationship between weight and lift

2 What do they agree may be an issue?
  A gathering accurate information
  B obtaining the materials
  C constructing the drone

Extract 2
You hear two friends discussing jackets that use smart technology.
3 What aspect of heated jackets do the man and woman disagree about?
  A whether they would be useful where the speakers are
  B how safe they might be in wet conditions
  C the reasons they are not very popular

4 What point does the man make about cooling jackets?
  A They are not very energy efficient.
  B They are uncomfortable to work in.
  C They may not be visually appealing.

Extract 3
You hear a man and woman discussing a science programme they watched on TV.
5 How does the woman feel about the helium balloon project?
  A unsure about its potential to help people
  B disappointed that it might not be a success
  C frustrated that the money has been wasted

6 What surprised the man in the second part of the programme?
  A that so few languages were represented on the internet.
  B that phone recycling schemes had not been tried before.
  C that relevant advice doesn't exist anywhere on the internet.

You are going to read an extract from a magazine article about the way science is communicated to the public. Six paragraphs have been removed from the extract. Choose from the paragraphs A–G the one which fits each gap (1–6). There is one extra paragraph which you do not need to use.

> **Exam advice**
>
> Look for ways of referring forwards and backwards at the beginnings and ends of paragraphs. These may include demonstrative pronouns (this, that, these, those) and comparative words (another, better, similar, the same, previous, etc.).

A Members of the public sitting down at such an event to gain information, discuss and make suggestions on the matter in hand is popular in many countries. In Denmark, for instance, Parliament is legally compelled to take note of the findings of this kind of gathering.

B One such artistic encounter with science is 'Root and Branch' or 'what trees can and can't do to address climate change', produced by the New Zealand media group 'Stuff'. This presentation explains land use, reforestation and climate change in Aotearoa, the Maori name for the country, with footage, text, pictures and infographics.

C It is unfortunate that these specific regulations were devised without any input from non-scientists, because they date back to a time when the importance of consultation with laypeople was not understood as fully as it is today.

D Examples of this include regulations on seatbelt use, which were drafted after consultation with those who had conducted research into the protection seatbelts offer in the event of collisions at different speeds. Similarly, levies on sugary foods were introduced based on the research findings of nutritionists.

E This thirst for scientific knowledge is generally viewed positively by the scientific community. One reason for this is that surveys have shown that as the field of science communication has grown, public trust in scientists has increased.

F Another such opportunity for active and interested people to get involved in is 'citizen science'. This allows volunteers to collect data as well as share their local knowledge, experience and skills with experts, who come into their communities for a genuine exchange of ideas.

G However, there are other, non-economic reasons to have non-scientists invested in science. Certain major global challenges, such as climate change, require the active involvement of individuals and communities, who have a key role to play in preventing environmental devastation. Similarly, information on nutrition and disease prevention needs to be widely disseminated.

Science communication

When most people think of a scientist, they probably picture someone in a white coat working in a laboratory, either alone or with other scientists. Unlike doctors, scientists do not traditionally have public-facing roles, but this is rapidly changing. Science communication is a fast-growing field, increasingly forming part of university science programmes, as a more educated public demands increasingly detailed information on scientific issues.

1 ....

A UK poll in 2019 revealed that 51% of people felt fairly well informed about science, up from 45% five years earlier. When presented with the negative statement, 'Science makes our way of life change too fast', only 27% agreed, about half the number who agreed with the same statement in 1996. Since in most countries, a large proportion of scientific research is funded by the taxpayer, it is vital to have public support and confidence in scientists.

2 ....

Scientists need to communicate their research in clear and simple terms, not just to the public but even more crucially, to decision-makers. In the UK, there are very few scientists in Parliament or even in the Civil Service, yet politicians are charged with developing policy based on scientific research. It is increasingly the case that governments appoint scientists to provide impartial advice, which will feed into new laws and policies.

3 ....

The majority of people will only take an interest in science if it is made entertaining. Therefore, science communicators put a great deal of effort into making it seem fascinating, attractive and cool. These days, science stories need to be truly immersive, with a mix of stunning photographs, video, illustrations and visual effects. These elements are often arranged in the most creative way possible, in order to engage a wide range of readers.

4 ....

However, science communication is not just about impressing people, or even keeping them informed. It is also concerned with setting up a dialogue between scientists and the public. The field has been grappling with the question of how to genuinely give the public a voice for several years. One option is consensus conferences, where a group of citizens are presented with evidence on a specific issue from experts and use what they have learnt to formulate recommendations.

5 ....

Elsewhere, rather than writing it into law, some funding organisations make engagement with laypeople a condition of providing research funding. Clearly, not everyone is going to be motivated to enter into dialogue with scientists. However, for those who are engaged, this is a chance to speak on behalf of non-scientists.

6 ....

While this kind of project has been criticised for exploiting laypeople by getting them to work as unpaid research assistants, overall, it is seen as a positive way to involve a wider section of the community in science. This and various other initiatives taken by science communicators have meant that careers in science are now viewed as exciting, future-focused and accessible to everyone.

Writing Part 1

An essay

Exam advice

Read through your essay carefully to ensure you have not repeated words and phrases. Instead, use synonyms, antonyms or paraphrase.

1 Read the Part 1 essay question. Make notes on each of the 3 ways to encourage young people to study STEM subjects. Which do you have more ideas about? Is there one idea which seems best to you?

Your class has attended a panel discussion on how to get more young people to study STEM (science, technology, engineering and maths) subjects. You have made the notes below.

> **Ideas to encourage young people to study STEM subjects**
>
> - Work experience
> - Educational visits
> - Financial incentives
>
> **Some opinions expressed in the discussion**
>
> 'Some young people are not aware of the careers available in STEM.'
>
> 'We need to inspire them with visits to museums and science centres.'
>
> 'Grants or bursaries should be given to students who choose STEM subjects.'

Write an essay discussing TWO of the ideas in your notes. You should explain which idea you think would be more successful in encouraging young people to study STEM subjects, giving reasons for your answer.

You may, if you wish, make use of the opinions expressed in the discussion, but you should use your own words as far as possible.

Write your **essay** in 220–260 words in an appropriate style.

2 Read the essay. Which of the three ideas listed in the question did the writer consider the best?

3 Complete the sentences with a word from the box to form a collocation.

> backgrounds industrial gain running required
> genuine decisions aside field opportunities

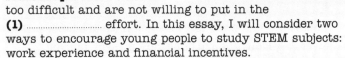

Discuss: How can we encourage young people to study STEM (science, technology, engineering and math) subjects at school?

Careers in science-related subjects can be extremely **rewarding**; however, many students **perceive** them as too difficult and are not willing to put in the **(1)** .... effort. In this essay, I will consider two ways to encourage young people to study STEM subjects: work experience and financial incentives.

Unless their families are involved in a scientific **(2)** .... , young people may be intimidated by workplaces such as laboratories and **(3)** .... plants. One way to get them involved is to **establish** relations between schools and employers, so that teenagers can **(4)** .... experience of STEM-based careers before they make **(5)** .... about further study. Schools could set **(6)** .... a few weeks of the year for students to observe and assist in relevant workplaces. In this way, they will have the opportunity to talk to scientists, engineers and technical workers about their jobs.

The second suggestion I would like to discuss is the idea of giving young people some kind of financial incentive to follow science-related careers. There are obvious advantages to this approach: in particular, it may **motivate** young people from disadvantaged **(7)** .... to **consider** a STEM-based career. However, in my personal opinion, there are dangers to this option. It may send a message that other careers are less valued. Furthermore, students may begin courses they are not really interested in, **(8)** .... the risk of more students not being able to **accomplish** what they set out to do.

On balance, schemes that allow young people to get experience of working in STEM-related careers would be the best way to encourage students with a **(9)** .... interest to understand what available **(10)** .... there are for them in these fields.

4 Look at the words in bold in the essay. Which word is NOT a synonym of the word on the left?

1	**rewarding**	satisfying	worthwhile	appropriate	fulfilling
2	**perceive**	regard	encourage	view	see
3	**establish**	appreciate	create	develop	form
4	**motivate**	encourage	drive	alter	inspire
5	**consider**	review	convince	examine	discuss
6	**accomplish**	achieve	launch	attain	complete

10 Learning for life

Grammar

Expressing ability, possibility and obligation

1 Find and correct the errors in seven of these sentences. The first one has been done for you.

1 You (mustn't) print your assignment in colour, but you can if you want to.
   don't have to

2 I could order the stationery for you if you had let me.

3 It was very kind of you to bring me a present, but you needn't have.

4 If we hadn't decided to go to the same university, we might never met.

5 It was difficult but in the end I could pass the exam.

6 Jack can have lost the office key. He was the last one to have it.

7 I must have attended today's lecture. I've missed three already.

8 Hopefully Roshani can able to retrieve your data for you.

2 Complete the second sentence so that it is a past tense form of the first sentence.

1 We don't have to wear a uniform at our school.
   We didn't have to wear a uniform
   at the first school I went to.

2 I can't understand my Maths teacher.
   When I was a child ....
   ....

3 Who's at the door? It must be Abdul.
   Who rang the doorbell at 11 pm? ....
   ....

4 Students must pay their fees before their exam results are released.
   When I was at school, ...
   .... before their exam results were released.

5 I can get hold of that book you need for your assignment.
   Look! I ....
   .... that book you needed for your assignment.

6 Frank might come to the party.
   Frank ....
   ...., but I didn't see him there.

7 Pupils mustn't talk while the teacher is talking.
   When I was a child, ...
   ....

Vocabulary

chance, occasion, opportunity and possibility

1 Circle the correct alternative in *italics* to complete the sentences.

1 There is a remote (*possibility*) / *opportunity* of the company being taken over.

2 We have to face the *possibility* / *occasion* of the conference being postponed.

3 There's an outside *opportunity* / *chance* that all three schools will merge.

4 We should view the school inspection as a golden *chance* / *opportunity* to show off the great work we're doing here.

5 Congratulations on your interview. You need to seize this *opportunity* / *possibility* with both hands.

6 I think we should allow Floyd to come back to school – after all, everyone deserves a second *chance* / *opportunity*.

7 When someone retires, we often mark the *opportunity* / *occasion* with a small party.

8 That was a brilliant performance. I think you're in with a *chance* / *possibility* of winning.

2 Complete the sentences using a phrase from the box.

> a distinct   ~~a sense of~~   an equal   arises   given the
> on one   on the off   rule out   welcome the

1 We asked the children to dress up to help create ....*a sense of*........ occasion.

2 Can you go to Mr Vincent's classroom .... chance that he has a few spare chairs?

3 The police just need to .... the possibility of family involvement in the crime.

4 The weather is terrible today. I'd stay at home too, ... chance.

5 Mara was always up to mischief. I remember .... occasion, she put a huge spider in the teacher's desk.

6 I'd like to study abroad if the opportunity ....

7 I've heard that there's .... possibility that the food technology course won't run next year.

8 I would .... chance to present my ideas to the governors.

9 We are .... opportunities employer, which means we consider all job applicants on their merits.

Listening Part 2

You will hear a lecture in which a man called Ajay Fernandez has been asked to talk about his time at a boarding school in Scotland. Complete the sentences with a word or short phrase.

For questions 1–8 complete the sentences with a word or short phrase.

Exam advice

Each question has its own short section of text, the start of which will be signalled in some way so you know you should start listening for the answer.

Being a pupil at St Stephen's Boarding School

1 It was mainly because of the .... that Ajay's parents chose St Stephen's School.

2 Ajay thought the school resembled a .... when he first saw it.

3 Ajay was taken aback by how .... Mr McEwan, the headmaster, was.

4 Ajay was pleased to find that there were .... in the room the boys slept in.

5 Ajay uses the word .... to describe his best friend, Gerry.

6 Of all the sports Ajay took part in, ... was his least favourite.

7 In Ajay's opinion, the .... was the best part of playing rugby matches at other schools.

8 Ajay suggests that the lack of .... was the main factor in his success in his studies.

Reading and Use of English Part 1

Read the text below and decide which answer (A, B, C or D) best fits each gap. There is an example at the beginning (0).

Example: (0)   A infers   B advises   C recommends   (D) suggests

Adaptive learning platforms

As the name **(0)** ....Ø......... , adaptive learning platforms 'adapt' to the individual needs of each learner. The key to their success is **(1)** .... as much data as possible, both before and during the learning process. Based on AI algorithms, this software **(2)** .... which lessons stick and which don't, so that teachers can **(3)** .... learning materials accordingly. Early studies have shown promising results. Platforms used at Arizona State University have **(4)** .... expectations. One study, for example, found that **(5)** .... from Maths courses have reduced by 47%.

Research in elementary schools, too, has revealed that adaptive learning platforms can help those who are behind and enrich the learning of those who are **(6)** .... Some platforms allow teachers to decide which specific skills students should master, or alternatively to **(7)** .... for student-driven education.

Proponents believe this approach suits the increasing diversity of the student population and many predict it will be the future of education. However, this way of learning is inevitably **(8)** .... on a reliable internet connection, something many schools, especially those in developing countries, still lack.

0	**A** infers	**B** advises	**C** recommends	**(D)** suggests		
1	**A** picking	**B** detecting	**C** gathering	**D** catching		
2	**A** ranks	**B** classifies	**C** determines	**D** tells		
3	**A** modify	**B** restore	**C** modernise	**D** renovate		
4	**A** outdone	**B** exceeded	**C** excelled	**D** overtaken		
5	**A** failures	**B** withdrawals	**C** resignations	**D** removals		
6	**A** before	**B** onwards	**C** forward	**D** ahead		
7	**A** opt	**B** select	**C** choose	**D** decide		
8	**A** controlled	**B** regulated	**C** contained	**D** dependent		

Exam advice

The missing words often form part of a phrase or collocation. When preparing for the exam, focus on 'chunks' of language and in Part 1 decide whether each gap forms part of a phrase or collocation with the words around it.

Reading and Use of English Part 8

You are going to read an extract from a blog in which four parents explain how they chose to educate their children. For questions 1–10, choose from the sections (A–D). The sections may be chosen more than once.

When preparing for the exam, try different approaches to this task. For example, try reading each text in detail and finding all the statements that match it. Then try skim reading all the texts and questions before attempting the questions in order to see which approach works best for you.

Exam advice

Which parent

took some time to make a decision about changes to their lifestyle?	1
has a different approach to teaching their children now from when they set out?	2
likes the fact that the method they have chosen covers only the core subjects?	3
references academic research to support their decisions.	4
chose a form of education based on their children's own needs?	5
implies that their children have a broad education?	6
had decided on their children's education in advance of becoming a parent?	7
considers formal education a kind of insurance policy for their children?	8
justifies delaying the start of their children's education?	9
suggests they are part of a movement of parents who share a point of view?	10

A   Simon Donaldson

Even before my children were born, my wife and I had decided not to send them to school. As older parents, we just wanted to spend more time with them and educate them ourselves. Yet our ideas about what homeschooling meant have changed beyond all recognition. We'd always known we wouldn't begin formal schooling until they were around 7 or 8, since research has shown there is no benefit to starting any younger. Although we started on a published curriculum, we soon abandoned it. Our elder son, Owen, had developed an interest in all things mechanical and we could see him learning through his own intrinsic curiosity. I ended up buying old cars and motorbikes for us to fix up together. By the age of 11, he had effectively completed an apprenticeship in car mechanics and had moved on to helping me rewire the house. Our second son, Byron, is more academic and loves anything to do with the natural world. Our children demonstrate that where education is concerned, one size doesn't fit all.

B   Tabitha Njoku

When my twin daughters, Rachel and Rebecca, landed roles in a major soap opera, we were concerned about how we would manage their education alongside rehearsals and filming. While we were thrilled by their sudden rise to fame, we were determined they would get a more or less traditional education and be ready for university in case the acting roles ever dried up. We heard about the Online High School from the father of another actor. Most of the other students are involved in performing arts or are seriously into a sport. Why it works for us is because they understand that these students have a limited amount of time to spend on schoolwork but still want to get the best results they can. The girls spend about 3 hours a day on essential subjects like maths, English and science so no time is wasted on 'fun' subjects as it would be in a normal school, but as the girls are doing something they love, and get plenty of interaction on set, that's not such a problem.

C   Michael Parsons

My children were six and eight when I was made redundant and decided to set up my own IT consulting company. My son, Damon, had never really settled at school and I was now in a position to take him out and teach him at home. My wife hadn't been enjoying her job for a while and everything just came together. She handed in her notice and started helping me in the business, taking over the homeschooling of Damon and our daughter, Rose. Suddenly, there was nothing tying us to one place. After much deliberation, we decided to rent out our house and buy a camper van. We became part of a growing 'world-schooling' community. Education really came alive for the children as we travelled around Europe. They learnt bits of different languages, and about the history, architecture, cuisine, and geography of all the places we visited. All sorts really. We occasionally meet up with other families who are doing the same thing and the children always find someone to play with.

D   Serena De Souza

Few are willing to accept that children, left to their own devices, will educate themselves. However, studies by experts have shown that this is the case. Of course, they have to be taught to read, write and do basic sums, but beyond that, it is a matter of making learning of various types accessible to them. Just as a child won't starve if you don't force-feed her, she won't grow up ignorant if you don't force a preordained curriculum onto her. I'd decided to homeschool before having my son and daughter, because I genuinely believe it is in their best interests and I had my own approach to children's education. What I do is order the study packs for subjects they've shown an interest in. In my experience, children won't learn anything that bores them, anyway, so why force them? We do plenty of hands-on learning and there are no set hours to the school day. If we travel a long way for a field trip, we sleep in the next day.

Writing Part 2
A report

> **Exam advice**
>
> Divide your report into sections with headings which address the points of the task, and avoid using informal language. The passive voice and noun phrases are two useful ways of making your writing more formal.

You recently completed a course to learn a practical skill. You have been asked to write a report for the director of the institute where you did the course. Your report should explain which aspects of the course you enjoyed most and which you found most beneficial. It should also make some recommendations for how the course could be improved.

1 Read the answer that a student called Samantha wrote for the exam task below. Read her response and decide if the statements are True (T) or False (F).

1 The response respects the word limit.
2 The report is divided into sections.
3 The headings are appropriate.
4 All three points given in the question are addressed.
5 All parts of the response are relevant.
6 The style is appropriate.
7 There is a wide range of vocabulary and sentence structure.

My report

Mr Morley asked me to write a report on the intensive driving course I recently took.

The course

The course lasted for one week (Monday to Friday) from 9am to 3pm. Each student had an instructor and a car of their own and there were five of us on the course. We all got on like a house on fire as we were all around the same age. One of the students, Molly, lived near the school so she went home every night. The rest of us came from different towns, so we stayed in a guest house. The guest house was pretty bad since dinner was at 6pm, which is much too early, and there was no choice at all. A few times we had to go and get pizza because the food was horrible.

Anyway, the course was good. We all liked the instructors because they were a good laugh. One day, it was so funny because one of the instructors, Bob was teaching us how to change a wheel. We were really struggling, and an old lady walked past and told him off for not helping us!

The end of the course

Out of five of us, three passed the driving test, which we took on the last day. Unfortunately, I failed. Still, it was a fun time and I have kept in touch with my mates from the course.

2 Match the phrases from Samantha's report with a more appropriate phrase.

1	like a house on fire	A	overall
2	pretty bad	B	extremely well
3	horrible	C	not very good
4	anyway	D	my friends
5	a good laugh	E	very amusing
6	so funny	F	fun to be with
7	my mates	G	the standard of food was inadequate

3 Samantha rewrote her report after receiving feedback from her teacher. Complete the noun phrases with a word from the box.

> unique   residential   dietary
> my own age   choice   self-catering
> tuition   maintenance   designated   nature

Purpose

The purpose of this report is to evaluate the one-week intensive driving course I recently took at Pass First Time driving school in Cheltenham.

Most enjoyable aspects

I thoroughly enjoyed my two-week intensive driving course. I particularly liked sharing the experience with a group of people (1) .... and, as it was a (2) .... course, spending the evenings together was great fun. Each of us was taught by a (3) .... instructor. Mine had a great sense of humour and praised me when I did well.

Most beneficial aspects

Having one-to-one (4) .... and remaining with the same instructor all week were extremely helpful aspects of the programme. Each instructor really got to know the strengths and weaknesses of their pupil and tailored their teaching to their needs. We were out on lessons all day, so the different aspects of driving became second (5) .... to us. We were offered the (6) .... of learning on a manual or an automatic car, which is a (7) .... feature of this programme. Since I was doing better than expected on an automatic, I was given the opportunity to change to a manual.

Recommendations

I would make three recommendations to improve the programme. Firstly, the school could consider using (8) .... accommodation. The guest house served dinner too early for most of us and there was no choice of food. The owner also didn't cater for special (9) .... requirements. Secondly, more emphasis should be placed on car (10) .... as we only had one session on this. Finally, some students suggested that more time could be spent on parking as this was what many students felt was their weakest skill.

4 Find five examples of the passive voice.

1 One in paragraph 2
2 Two in paragraph 3
3 Two in paragraph 4

11 Globetrotters

Vocabulary

Fixed phrases

1 Match 1–8 with a–h to make phrases.

1	out in	a	your cool
2	get sick	b	point of
3	keep	c	fortune on
4	without	d	waiting
5	spend a	e	the open
6	rough	f	and tired of
7	the whole	g	it
8	be kept	h	a trace

2 Replace the words in bold with a phrase from Exercise 1. Make any other necessary changes.

1 Susanna **paid a lot of money for** that Caribbean cruise. *spent a fortune on*

2 **The only reason we chose** to go to South America was for Nathan to practise his Spanish.

3 We had to **put up with bad conditions** on our school camping trip – we slept on the floor and there was no running water.

4 I work in an office, so when I get free time, I need to be **in the fresh air**.

5 Jaime can't **stay calm** in a crisis, so I don't think I'd like to go travelling with him.

6 My sister is a flight attendant and she says she **gets fed up with** rude passengers.

7 My favourite travel bag has **completely and utterly** disappeared.

8 I hate **it when people make me wait**.

at, in and *on* to express location

3 Complete the table with the phrases in the box.

> Asia   a party   a queue   an island
> the moon   the outskirts   the phone
> the surroundings   ~~the top floor~~   work

at	in	on
		the top floor

4 Complete the extract from a travel blog with *at*, *in* or *on*.

For me, Spain is one of the most beautiful countries (1) .... Europe. However, you won't find me (2) .... the coast with the other British tourists. In my opinion, some of the most interesting places can be found (3) .... the middle of the country. In fact, one place I visited (4) .... Castilla-La Mancha is probably one of the most fascinating places (5) .... Earth. Situated (6) .... a distance of about 25 km from the city of Cuenca is Ciudad Encantada or the Enchanted City. The area consists of dozens of rock formations in striking shapes. As rain fell (7) .... the limestone plateau, it wore down the porous limestone, leaving behind the stronger rock. (8) .... the entrance to the city is a giant's head keeping guard. My Spanish friends and I visited (9) .... sunset and had a picnic (10) .... the forest. (11) .... the magical atmosphere of Ciudad Encantada, I could imagine myself (12) .... a different millennium or even (13) .... a different planet.

Grammar

Conditionals

1 Choose the correct option. In some sentences, both may be correct. If both are correct, what is the difference in meaning?.

1 If every day was a holiday, we *'d* / *'ll* soon get bored of it.

2 We *'d be lying* / *'d lie* on the beach right now if we hadn't missed the flight.

3 If we *were getting* / *get* out of here alive, I'll never take another risk in my life.

4 Nowadays my parents don't travel unless it *'s* / *will be* to stay at a luxurious resort.

5 If you'd been respectful to the guide, he *wouldn't have left* / *wouldn't be leaving* without us.

6 Becca *would choose* / *would have chosen* the environmentally friendly option if it were more affordable.

7 Unless I *were* / *'m* mistaken, the hostel is this way.

8 If you*'d been* / *'re* resourceful enough, you can survive even in the harshest of environments.

9 If I hadn't been running, I *wouldn't be* / *wouldn't have been* out of breath.

10 I'm not going on the office trip unless it *'s* / *isn't* better organised than last time.

11 I *would* / *could* appreciate it if you would take off your shoes before entering the temple.

wish and *if only*

2 Complete the sentences with the correct form of the verb in brackets. Make the verb negative if necessary.

1 If only I ....had......... enough money to go on holiday this year. (have)

2 I wish I .... so much chocolate. I feel sick.(eat)

3 I wish I .... what the time was. (know)

4 If only I .... so much on Christmas presents. I'm broke now! (spend)

5 I wish the weather .... (improve)

6 If only I .... Italian. I'd know what they were saying about me. (speak)

7 I wish we .... the flight earlier. The prices have gone up. (book)

8 I wish I .... in a flat. It would be lovely to have a garden. (live)

9 If only my dad .... criticising me. (stop)

Reading and Use of English Part 2

> Read the whole text before you begin. Read it through again when you've finished to check whether it makes sense. | **Exam advice**

Read the text below and think of the word which best fits each gap. Use only one word in each gap. There is an example at the beginning (0).

Hovercrafts

Example (0): other

The hovercraft is an amphibious vehicle - in **(0)** ....other......... words, it can travel on land like a bus and on water like a boat, though **(1)** .... of these modes of transport could be said to be as exciting as a hovercraft. It has more in common with a plane, what with a journey by hovercraft also **(2)** .... referred to as a 'flight'.

Powerful fans blow air under the hovercraft, lifting **(3)** .... between 15 cm and 2.1 metres off the ground. A hovercraft's base is covered by a fabric 'skirt', which **(4)** .... only prevents the air escaping but also helps the vehicle avoid obstacles.

All over the world, the hovercraft's ability to handle rough terrain **(5)** .... it a popular choice with the military. Hovercrafts are also used **(6)** .... place of boats. This is on **(7)** .... of them not needing as much time to cover the same distance. The Isle of Wight, off the south coast of the UK, **(8)** .... home to the world's only commercial hovercraft service.

Listening Part 1

> Make sure you are used to listening to speakers with a wide range of accents in as many different contexts as possible. This will make it easier to tune into each speaker's accent or way of talking. | **Exam advice**

12 You will hear three different extracts. Choose the answer (A, B or C) which fits best according to what you hear. There are two questions for each extract.

Extract 1

You hear a husband and wife comparing two holiday resorts.

1 What does the woman like about the resort they are staying at now?

A the attentiveness of the staff

B the convenient location

C the quiet and relaxing atmosphere

2 What point does the man make about the resort they stayed in last year?

A They ended up spending more money on extras.

B The meals were not as bad as the woman suggests.

C It allowed for more spontaneous activities.

Extract 2

You hear a man and a woman talking about occasions they went travelling.

3 What is the woman doing during the conversation about Thailand?

A describing an interesting aspect of the country she visited

B complaining about the standard of her accommodation

C highlighting to an element of her holiday she found satisfactory

4 When talking about his trip around Europe the man is

A illustrating the benefit of a chance encounter.

B criticising the actions of another traveller.

C expressing regret regarding a missed opportunity.

Extract 3

You hear two friends discussing a travel trend called 'glamping', a style of camping.

5 Which aspect of glamping does the woman not understand?

A the kinds of accommodation that define it as 'glamping'

B the reasons glamping appeals to some people

C how the prices compare with other types of holiday

6 What point does the man make about glamping?

A He prefers the tents used in traditional camping.

B It's mainly a trick to make money from tourists.

C The locations used are better than traditional campsites.

Writing Part 2

A review

1 Read the review below and answer the questions.

1 Who is the review for?
2 What is the purpose of the review?
3 Does it include both positive and negative points?

Let's go! Amsterdam

When I first booked my trip to Amsterdam, I was overwhelmed by the number of online travel guides out there so I hope this impartial review of *Let's go* will help others decide which one to use.

My first impression of the site was a positive one as from the landing page, I was able to click through to the site's enticing homepage without having to sign up to receive updates. I was immediately attracted by the stunning photos, and the clever design makes navigation around the site easy.

Unlike some other guides I tried, the options menu is logical and user-friendly. In addition to the descriptions of the city's main attractions, there were links to each one, enabling the visitor to book easily. The sidebar contained links to related sites, such as airlines, hotels and car hire companies. While this is a potentially useful feature, unfortunately several of the links I clicked on were broken.

Let's go is linked to several fascinating travel blogs, which I found really informative. One was written by a British man living in Amsterdam and I picked up some great tips from him. The only complaint I have is that the links to the blogs could be easily missed as you had to scroll right down to the bottom of the homepage.

Overall, *Let's go* is an easy-to-use site, jam-packed with helpful advice for visitors to Amsterdam and other European cities. While a few technical problems remain, it is constantly improving and I highly recommend it for business travellers and tourists alike.

2 Before writing the above review, the student wrote a plan. Match the points A–E to the paragraphs of the review.

A Summary
B Features and layout
C Purpose of the review
D Blogs
E My initial thoughts on the site

3 Find words related to websites with the following meanings.

1 a webpage which serves as an entry point for a website (paragraph 2)
2 to select one or more links to move to another webpage (paragraph 2)
3 a webpage which contains introductory information about a website (paragraph 2)
4 finding your way to different pages within a website (paragraph 2)
5 a list of choices on a website (paragraph 3)
6 a box at the edge of a homepage showing less important content (paragraph 3)
7 a word, phrase or image that takes you to another webpage or website (paragraph 3)
8 a regularly updated, informal website, usually written by an individual (paragraph 4)
9 to move down the screen (paragraph 4)

Reading and Use of English Part 5

You are going to read a magazine article about 'staycations'. Choose the answer (A, B, C, D) which you think fits best according to the text.

1 What do the words 'that fact' (line 13) refer to?
   A the sudden increase in holidays within the UK
   B the person's recent trip within the UK
   C the lack of value placed on staycations
   D the reply the writer gave to the person

2 The main purpose of the second paragraph is to
   A show how quickly the travel industry grew.
   B illustrate the lack of facilities in the early resorts.
   C criticise the inequalities in society in the past.
   D explain that few people travelled until recently.

3 What does the writer suggest about British holiday resorts in paragraph 3?
   A They are a valued part of the country's culture.
   B Working-class people didn't benefit from them.
   C They were spoilt by the development of trains.
   D They are understandably no longer popular.

4 According to the writer, why did Butlins holiday camps attract so many visitors?
   A The accommodation was better quality than at other camps.
   B They were much cheaper than most other holiday camps.
   C There were no extra expenses for holidaymakers.
   D There were the only camps which had entertainment facilities.

5 In paragraph 5, the writer implies that holiday camps declined in popularity because

  A people wanted more freedom when they were on holiday.

  B they stopped being attractive to younger holidaymakers.

  C they weren't successful at keeping up with new trends.

  D they didn't allow people to bring their own vehicles.

6 Overall, the writer of the text expresses the view that

  A foreign holidays are preferable to staycations.

  B the UK is under-appreciated by the British.

  C British resorts need to cater better to tourists.

  D workers in the UK do not have enough holidays.

The history of the staycation

It says a lot that the recent trend of spending a few days somewhere else in the UK has had to be given its own fancy name. Calling it a staycation (stay+vacation) not only makes it feel like something people have never done before, but also shows how we compare it to our now frequent trips abroad. A colleague told me that he 'needed a holiday', following his week on the English coast. This was followed by, 'Oh that doesn't count' when that fact was pointed out. In the late 20th and early 21st century, we became so used to jetting off to exotic locations on a whim, that nowadays we barely consider it a break if it doesn't involve going through customs and immigration. Not only has this almost ubiquitous travel bug caused serious harm to the planet, it has also left many of our own wonderful seaside resorts a shadow of their former selves.

Those bemoaning the lack of opportunity for foreign travel should remember that the vast majority of people who have ever lived never travelled more than a few miles from their birthplace. In the Middle Ages, the only reasons to travel were work, war or pilgrimage to religious shrines. In the UK in 16th and 17th centuries, it was common for young men from wealthy backgrounds to take a 'grand tour' of Europe to round off their education, but the vast majority would still never leave their local area. The 18th century saw the rise in popularity of spas in towns such as Bath and Tunbridge Wells, where the upper classes would go to 'take the waters'. Gradually lodging houses for visitors to stay, coffee houses, shops and recreational facilities like bowling greens grew up around the spas as a precursor to the modern holiday resort.

From the mid-19th century, the coming of the railways led to a huge increase in the number of people heading towards Britain's seaside towns. Doctors extolled the virtues of sea air and salt water for good physical well-being. While the rich took to spending weeks or months by the sea to recuperate after an illness, the poor still only had a few days' holiday a year. The new railway companies were geared towards these day-trippers, who could now get from London to a coastal resort and back in one day. Historic photographs show 'bathing machines' along the shoreline. These huts on wheels were for ladies to preserve their modesty while changing and entering the water. The tradition of the great British seaside holiday was born, the essential ingredients of which included seafood such as jellied eels and whelks, funny hats, sandcastles and deckchairs.

The development of the seaside holidays mirrored the progress of workers'

rights. In 1939, a law was passed to give all workers one week's paid holiday a year and by the 1950s, most workers got two. This period saw the rise of the holiday camp. Billy Butlin, whose first camp opened in 1936, wanted to make a 'luxurious and affordable fantasy world' for working class people. The massive success of the Butlin's brand can be attributed to two main factors: the lure of the all-inclusive concept and the fact that the camps were 'weather-proof'. The British weather regularly ruined people's precious week off work, but at Butlin's the ample covered spaces – gymnasiums, reading rooms, theatres and even funfairs – meant that, as Billy himself put it, 'You cannot spend a single dull moment'.

Holiday camps had their own culture, which older Britons look back on with fondness. Despite the fun to be had, they were rather regimented places, with 'campers' being woken up at 8am by music and daily announcements from the site's many loudspeakers. Similarly, many seaside guest houses tended to be run by inflexible landladies with strict rules. It's no surprise that in the latter part of the 1960s, as more families got their own cars, camping and caravanning holidays became all the rage.

Holidays abroad became a possibility for an increasing number of UK residents throughout the 70s and 80s. 1979 was the first year that Britons spent more on overseas holidays than they did on holidays in the UK. The opening of the Channel Tunnel in 1994 connected England and France by rail, and the launch of budget airlines in 1995 made international travel cheaper and home-based tourism less attractive. Many young people born in the 1990s have spent more holidays in foreign hot spots than in our own beautiful UK tourist resorts. But if the current trend continues, that situation may no longer be the case and the staycation might be here to stay.

12 Our planet

Vocabulary

Prepositions following verbs

1 Complete the sentences with the correct form of a verb from box A and a preposition from box B. You can use the prepositions more than once.

A

apologise	apply	attach
contribute	~~depend~~	focus
incorporate	insist	protest

B

against	for
into	on	to

1 People on the plains .... their animals for their livelihood.
2 We .... any inconvenience caused by the late departure of your flight.
3 As you can see, the important elements of the previous logo .... the new one.
4 Nowadays wildlife organisations .... empowering local communities to protect their own land.
5 The students were .... the government's decision not to promote renewable energy production.
6 After graduating, Rosie .... several international corporations, but in the end, she took a local job.
7 Nick .... sitting in the front of the jeep when he was on safari last week.
8 We .... the trailer .... the back of our car.
9 Would you like to .... Leah's leaving present?

Word formation

2 Are the words in bold used correctly? If not, correct them.

1 We are **honour** that you could be with us today, Dr Watson.
2 My uncle is very keen on **birdwatch**. He goes every weekend.
3 The government has ordered an **investigating** into the incident.
4 We are determined to hold the offenders **accountable** for their actions.
5 Many **city-dwell** children have never seen an animal in the wild.
6 These days people spend less time **outdoor** than they did in the past.
7 I've never experienced **firsthanded** the thrill of seeing an elephant in its natural habitat.
8 There were no **see-witnesses** to the crime.
9 I think some so-called green products are a bit of a **rip-on**.
10 Litter picking is quite **time-consuming** but it makes you feel great.
11 The event will be more successful if we can get a **high-profiling** guest speaker.

Grammar

Articles

1 Complete the extract from an article about sloths by adding *a/an*, *the* or *Ø* (no article).

(1) .... sloths are creatures of habit, highly adapted for (2) .... life high up in the canopy of tropical rainforests. In fact, they usually have (3) .... little need to go down to ground level. Native to (4) .... South and Central America, sloths are threatened by (5) .... destruction of their natural habitat.

(6) .... organisation called the Sloth Conservation Foundation has been set up to protect sloths. One of (7) .... main functions of this organisations is to educate local people and teach them to live harmoniously alongside sloths. People anywhere in (8) .... world can adopt (9) .... sloth. Of course, this doesn't mean that they can take (10) .... sloth home with them! Instead, they will receive (11) .... fascinating book called *Life in the fast lane* by Dr Rebecca Cliffe, as well as lots of (12) .... other interesting gifts. This would be (13) .... great birthday or Christmas present for (14) .... animal lover.

Countable and uncountable nouns

2 Decide if the nouns in bold are used correctly. If they are not, correct them.

1 My job involves giving **advices** to businesses on how to be greener.
2 There is a lot of false **informations** on the internet.
3 I have increased my **knowledge** of wildlife conservation.
4 In my town, there are lots of different types of **accommodation**.
5 Most French families buy **breads** every morning.
6 It's recommended that you eat five types of **fruit** and vegetables every day.
7 Budget airlines only allow carry-on **baggages**.
8 **Travel** broadens the mind.
9 The audience gave the singer a round of **applause**.
10 The hurricane did a great deal of **damages** to the power lines.

Writing Part 2
A proposal

Focus on the use of future forms in your proposal. Tenses such as the past simple, present perfect and present continuous may be used in the introductory section.

Exam advice

1 Read the task. How would you answer this? Then read the model answer and compare it to your ideas

You see this advertisement on the local council website.

Have you been down to the beach lately? Then you will know that we need a massive clean-up operation. We are looking for proposals on ways to clean up our beaches. In your proposal, you should suggest who could organise and help with the clean-up, when and how it could happen and how it could be funded.

Write your proposal in 220–260 words.

2 Read the model answer again and choose the correct word or phrase.

3 Match the tenses with the reasons for using them.

1 future simple
2 *going to* future
3 first conditional
4 future continuous
5 *can* + infinitive

a to talk about the future consequence of a likely possibility
b to express future predictions
c to express future possibility
d to express future intentions
e to talk about an action in progress at a specified time in the future

4 Find an example of each tense from Exercise 3 in the given paragraph.

1 future simple (paragraph 3)
2 *going to* future (paragraph 2)
3 first conditional (paragraph 2)
4 future continuous (paragraph 3)
5 *can* + infinitive (paragraph 4)

5 Find words in the text which mean:

1 a useful or valuable skill, quality or person (paragraph 1)
2 to explain clearly, usually in writing (paragraph 1)
3 the careful use of valuable natural substances (paragraph 2)
4 improve the quality of (paragraph 2)
5 money given by an organisation for an event or activity (paragraph 4)
6 activities that are planned to achieve something (paragraph 4)
7 to do or begin to do something, especially something difficult (paragraph 4)
8 the fact that you own something (paragraph 5)

Purpose

Our beaches are some of this country's greatest assets, attracting thousands of visitors each year. **(1)** *A few years ago / In recent years*, they have become polluted with debris washing in from the sea and litter left behind by locals and tourists. The purpose **(2)** *of / for* this proposal is to lay out my ideas for cleaning up our beautiful coastline.

People

The beaches belong to all of us. **(3)** *Therefore / However*, my proposal is to involve a wide range of people across the country. If my proposal is accepted, I will partner with schools and involve students, who will learn about conservation and social responsibility. **(4)** *On the other hand / Similarly*, I would like to invite businesses to contribute one day a year of each employee's time to help with the clean-up. **(5)** *In exchange / In this way*, they can advertise this on their website to enhance their reputation.

When and how

Schools, businesses and clubs will be cleaning the beaches on days and times convenient to them. Volunteers will co-ordinate their efforts. Grabbing tools, gloves and refuse sacks will be provided to all participants **(6)** *so that / in order to* facilitate this work. **(7)** *As a result / In addition*, posters will invite tourists to pick up three pieces of litter during their visit and equipment will be made available to them to do this.

Funding

Funding will be required for the purchase of the above-mentioned equipment. I would like to request that part of the cost be met by the council. **(8)** *During / While* major clean-up operations, we will undertake the collection of donations from the public. Contributions can also be made through the council website.

Conclusion

This is a low-cost proposal, which has the added advantage of creating a sense of ownership among local communities.

Listening Part 2

 13 You will hear a conservationist called Emma Bradshaw giving a talk to a group of students on career opportunities in wildlife conservation. For questions 1–8, complete the sentences with a word or short phrase.

Careers in wildlife conservation

1 Emma gained work experience by helping out at a .... when she was studying.

2 Emma explains that .... are the best way of getting into the field of conservation.

3 Emma mentions a course in .... which would suit those who want practical job-oriented training.

4 Emma explains that she was most interested in working with .... when she started her first zoo job.

5 Emma's second position at the zoo was working in the .... for five years.

6 When Emma worked in Gabon, it was the .... that she found most challenging.

7 Emma tells the students that jobs related to .... are often available in the field of conservation.

8 Emma gives the example of managing .... as a job which supports people working in the field of conservation.

Reading and Use of English Part 7

You are going to read an extract from a magazine article about jaguars – a type of panther. Six paragraphs have been removed from the extract. Choose from the paragraphs A–G the one which fits each gap (1–6). There is one extra paragraph which you do not need to use.

A The jaguar's range – that is the area it travels through – provides more than 53 million people with ecosystem services, including fresh water, commercial fisheries, clean air and crop pollination. In Brazil alone, these crucial services generate $4 billion per year.

B In this way, the poachers benefit from the poverty of villagers, who will happily kill jaguars for the large sums of money on offer. Unscrupulous people use community radio stations and public spaces to offer these tempting rewards.

C This is a complex issue. Even though agricultural workers may understand the importance of jaguar conservation, they are unlikely to prioritise it over feeding their families. Panthera, the only organisation devoted solely to big cats, is now working alongside other NGOs to promote peaceful land sharing between cattlemen and jaguars.

D Another innovative method has been introduced by the Instituto Nacional de Tecnologia Agropecuaria (INTA) in Argentina. They use sheepdogs, raised from puppyhood alongside the sheep, to guard the livestock. The dogs develop such a strong bond with the sheep that they protect them like family and deter predators.

E In fact, the jaguar is soon going to labelled 'Vulnerable' on the International Union for the Conservation of Nature (IUCN) Red List. Half of their historic territory has been lost, though in some areas of Brazil, Paraguay and Argentina that figure rises to 85%.

F Part of this plan is the jaguar corridor project, which seeks to protect jaguars across a 6 million km2 range. The aim is to preserve the genetic integrity of the species by offering safe passage to jaguars so they can mate with other populations.

G Another tribe, the Olmecs, who flourished in Mexico in the Pre-Christian era, worshipped a deity known as a 'werejaguar', a half human and half jaguar supernatural entity. This symbolises the close connection between humans and jaguars throughout history.

Jaguar conservation

The jaguar, or Panthera Onca, is the largest cat in the Americas. The name 'jaguar' comes from the TupÍ- GuaranÍ word, Yaguara, which means 'he who kills in one leap'. For thousands of years, the jaguar has had important mythological and cultural significance among indigenous communities. The Mayans associated the jaguar with the afterlife, believing it could move between the living and the dead.

1 ....

Nevertheless, the crucial role of the jaguar in Central and South America is not simply cultural, but practical too. The jaguar is an 'umbrella species'. Occupying a position at the top of the food chain, it has a positive impact on the entire ecosystem. In a region with a thriving jaguar population, all biodiversity will be healthy. This is because the jaguar's prey and the forest need to be in good condition for the jaguar itself to survive.

2 ....

However, that country is far from being the only one the jaguar inhabits. In the past, jaguars roamed freely from Argentina to the southern United States. They are now extinct in El Salvador and Uruguay, and Panama's rapid industrial development has created an impassable obstacle, preventing interaction and mating among different populations of jaguars. This clearly impacts on their health and survival as a species.

3 ....

Reasons for this destruction of habitat are obvious. Increased demand for beef and soya (mainly as animal feed) have led to deforestation. However, it is not just the reduction in their range that has decimated jaguar populations. During the 1960s and 70s, 18,000 jaguars a year were killed for their fur and body parts. While wildlife protection laws have reduced those numbers, jaguars are still killed by ranchers in order to protect their livestock and their own livelihoods.

4 ....

These experts realise that practical solutions are the key to co-existence. They train farmers in anti-predator husbandry techniques, such as the use of electric fences and enclosures to keep their animals safe overnight when jaguars hunt. Another solution is to place tough water buffalo in with the cattle as a deterrent, and farmers have even been supported to breed stronger 'battle cattle' that are more resilient to attack.

5 ....

In addition to providing such non-lethal solutions to the issue of jaguar attacks, organisations have been working on pan-American initiatives to preserve jaguars across the continent. Jaguar 2030 Roadmap is a joint project of WWF and others to secure 30 priority jaguar conservation landscapes by 2030. Focusing on one species across several countries allows for a more targeted approach.

6 ....

There are early signs that this intense effort on behalf of this emblematic species is paying off. In Mexico, for example, the jaguar population has doubled since 2002. In Yucatan peninsula, 600 jaguars live in the Calakmul Biosphere Reserve, a green paradise where they are protected. The current joined-up thinking of conservationists working across national borders seems likely to offer even greater protection to jaguars.

13 A healthy lifestyle

Vocabulary

Prepositions following adjectives

1 Complete the extract from a lifestyle blog with prepositions. The first one has been done for you.

Like most people, I'm fully aware **(1)** ......of...... what I should be doing to support my well-being. However, in common **(2)** .... many of you, I don't always do it. Are you tired **(3)** .... feeling that it's all too much? I was, and I'm not suggesting you don't know any of what I'm going to tell you. I used to be intolerant **(4)** .... people who told me I needed to get more sleep, do more exercise and eat better. But the thing is, all of those are absolutely critical **(5)** .... our physical and emotional health. Until recently, I was obsessed **(6)** .... being the first in the office in the morning. I was devoted **(7)** .... my job without realising how damaging my poor diet and lack of sleep were **(8)** .... every aspect of my life, including my work. Although I was exhausted, I suffered from insomnia and I was anxious **(9)** .... even very minor problems. Right now, I'm sleeping more, exercising more and eating better and I'm proud **(10)** .... what I've achieved. However, we all need frequent reminders about being kind to ourselves and I, like most of you, am capable **(11)** .... falling into bad habits again.

2 Complete the sentences with an adjective from the box and a preposition.

> acceptable   closed   confident   delighted
> familiar   frustrated   responsible   sensitive   suited

1 This destructive pattern of behaviour may be .... some of you.
2 The swimming pool is .... non-members this morning.
3 Tai Chi is a gentle type of exercise that is perfectly .... older people.
4 I'm .... your decision to join our gym.
5 Ana is .... her chances in the gymnastics tournament.
6 Each one of us is .... our own health and well-being. We can't blame others for our poor choices.
7 I always wear a T-shirt on the beach as my skin is very .... the sun.
8 I keep forgetting the steps to the new dance and I'm very .... it.
9 The sports centre's new membership policy was not .... the committee so they expressed their objection to it.

3 Find and correct the errors in six of these sentences. The first one has been done for you.

1 Our teacher was **proud ~~about~~** our exam results.   *of*
2 I'm **disappointed in** myself- I could have won the race if I'd trained harder.
3 Nisha is **anxious with** her meeting with her boss tomorrow.
4 My roses are not doing too well. I don't think they're **suited in** this climate.
5 I've just finished decorating my bedroom and I'm really **pleased with** the way it's turned out.
6 Try to be **kind with** everyone, you might need their help one day.
7 Dan was so **confident at** passing his driving test that he had organised a party to celebrate.
8 I'm usually quite **tolerant at** noisy neighbours but last night's party was too much even for me.

Grammar

Ways of contrasting ideas

1 Choose the correct option in *italics*.

1 *Although / Despite* having a car, Justin tends to walk everywhere.

2 *In spite of / Even though* I do a lot of exercise, I'm not that strong.

3 *Whereas / Despite* following all the advice, I still suffer from insomnia.

4 Juan prefers team sports, *whereas / however* I prefer individual sports.

5 The doctor thought my ankle might be fractured *but / despite* in the end it was just a sprain.

6 Darcy is a very early riser. She has a lie-in at the weekend, *though / although*.

7 *But / While* I agree with veganism in principle, it is quite a hard lifestyle to maintain.

8 I eat healthily during the week. *However / Even though*, I tend to eat junk food at the weekend.

9 *Although / However* pollution is decreasing slightly, it is still affecting people's health.

2 Add the word in brackets in the correct place. Join the sentences together where possible.

1 Ollie does a lot of sport. His twin brother prefers to watch. (whereas)

   Whereas Ollie does a lot of sport, his twin brother prefers to watch.

2 All my family suffer from allergies. I seem to have escaped. (however)

3 Sofia enjoys skiing holidays. Delfina prefers lying on the beach. (while)

4 My grandmother is 95 years old. She still does her own housework. (despite)

5 My sister has asthma. It's not as bad as it used to be. (but)

6 Colin and Jill live in the countryside. They go to London every week. (though)

7 I had a nice hot bath last night. My muscles ache. (even though)

8 Alfredo is extroverted. His sister Catherine is introverted. (whereas)

9 I take vitamins every day. I still catch a lot of colds. (although)

The language of comparison

3 Use the prompts and the words in brackets to make comparative sentences. Make any other necessary changes.

1 I / spend / time / reading / now / past (much more)

   I spend much more time reading now than I did in the past.

2 My house / not / well designed / yours (as … as)

3 We / get / days off / other employees (fewer)

4 Emilie / not / do / activities / her sister (as many)

5 This book / becoming / interesting (more and more)

6 Simon / best / skier / team (by far)

7 Second TV series / not / funny / first (nearly as)

8 Tracey / expert / me (more of)

9 Jake / make / effort / other students (less)

4 Find and correct the errors in six of these sentences. The first one has been done for you.

1 Sarah is more of active than the rest of the family.

   Sarah is more ~~of~~ active than the rest of the family.

2 The north of Scotland is by far colder than the south of England.

3 It is much more better to give than to receive.

4 Children today don't have as much books as children in the past.

5 This is the worse birthday I've ever had!

6 Most annoyingly of all, I forgot to order the food for the party.

7 The winters are getting more and more hot every year.

8 Running isn't as nearly as good for you as swimming.

9 Most people say French is a bit more difficult to learn than Spanish.

Reading and Use of English Part 3

Read the text below. Use the word given in capitals at the end of some of the lines to form a word that fits in the gap in the same line. There is an example at the beginning (0).

Write your answers IN CAPITAL LETTERS

Example (0): POSSESSIONS

The minimalist lifestyle

Do you have lots of beautiful **(0)** POSSESSIONS, but still aren't content? Maybe you should consider a minimalist lifestyle.	**POSSESS**
The concept is based on the idea that 'less is more' and aims to avoid **(1)** .... consumerism – an issue that blights many of our lives. The **(2)** .... of minimalism is to value experiences over objects and avoid the stress that can come from **(3)**	**EXCESS** **BASE** **OWN**
Consider the reasons you have so much. How much of your purchasing was down to peer **(4)** ....? For many, because of the extreme materialism of the modern world, it's **(5)** .... to just buy the things they need.	**PRESS** **THINK**
Another reason why people adopt a minimalist lifestyle is to achieve **(6)** .... of mind. They find that uncluttering their house creates space in their head.	**CLEAR**
The minimalist lifestyle is not just about minimising what you own. It can also involve minimising your **(7)** .... so that you have the time to do the things you want. Most people who have tried this way of life have found it **(8)** .... liberating.	**COMMIT** **CREDIBLE**

Listening Part 3

You will hear an interview in which two practitioners of holistic well-being, called Shalini Anand and Darren Peterson are talking about their work. For questions 1–6, choose the answer (A, B, C or D) which fits best according to what you hear.

1 What does Shalini say about holistic well-being's connection to alternative medicine?
   A Only some types of alternative medicine relate closely to holistic well-being.
   B Alternative medicine and holistic well-being have similar underlying beliefs.
   C The two areas have been closely linked for a long time.
   D The connection between the two is more widely understood nowadays.

2 What does Shalini say about the different elements of well-being?
   A She believes that mental and emotional well-being are very similar.
   B Modern practitioners agree that there are five elements to holistic well-being.
   C Not all elements are recognised by the medical community.
   D There has been a growth in interest in spiritual well-being.

3 What does Shalini explain about the relationship between holistic and conventional medicine?

   A Holistic and conventional approaches should rarely be used in tandem.

   B Holistic practitioners understand that patients can benefit from recognised medical practices.

   C Few holistic practitioners have a background in conventional medicine.

   D Healthcare professionals are increasingly dismissive of holistic approaches.

4 What does Darren consider the most important step people can take towards well-being?

   A ignore what you see on social media

   B devote more time to healthy pursuits

   C prioritise your relationships with your loved ones

   D practise being more self-assured about who you are

5 What is the main reason Darren talks about goji berries?

   A to emphasise the importance of good nutrition

   B to suggest that not all fruit is equally healthy

   C to discourage the purchasing of imported food

   D to illustrate how the benefits of some products are oversold

6 What point does Darren want to make about holistic well-being when he mentions his grandmother?

   A that people in the past didn't need it as much.

   B that it was important before people knew about it.

   C that those with few means struggle to achieve it.

   D that she taught him what she knew about it.

Writing Part 2

A letter

> Even if you are writing to complain about something, you should remain polite. It is still possible to express your ideas powerfully.
>
> **Exam advice**

 1 Read a student's response to a Part 2 (letter) task. For 1–10, choose the more appropriate word or phrase.

2 Match the linking words and phrases in the box to a word or phrase in bold in the letter.

> consequently   this will mean that
> to begin with   including   frankly
> in addition   now that
> bearing in mind

Dear Mr Everett

I'm writing to explain why I feel the school is not **(1)** *currently* / *right now* doing enough to **(2)** *promote* / *push for* healthy lifestyles among the **(3)** *people* / *student body* and to make some suggestions regarding changes that could be **(4)** *made* / *implemented*.

Firstly, I would like to **(5)** *refer you to* / *tell you about* some research that has been conducted on the importance of healthy living for children and teenagers. It has been found that adolescents who eat a diet rich in fruit, vegetables and wholegrains, sleep at least eight hours a night and exercise three or more times a week are 80% more likely to succeed in examinations than the average student. **Given** these statistics, promoting healthy living should **(6)** *come first* / *be an absolutely priority* for our school.

To be frank, I find it **(7)** *alarming* / *disgusting* that PE lessons have been reduced from three to one per week. Not only that, but where timetable clashes occur, PE is always the first to be dropped in favour of academic subjects, and **as a result**, many students are not exercising regularly. **What is more**, the school canteen still sells mainly unhealthy processed foods **such as** chicken nuggets, pizza and chips.

I suggest **(8)** *rethinking* / *thinking again* about the school calendar to include charity walks, runs or swims and **(9)** *lots more types* / *a wider variety* of team sports. **In this way**, there will be at least one healthy activity which appeals to everyone. **Since** the benefits of a largely plant-based diet have now been proven, there needs to be an increase in the number of meat-free options available in the canteen. Alongside this, assemblies and citizenship lessons should educate students in all aspects of a healthy lifestyle.

(10) I *appreciate* / *Thanks for* your attention on this matter.

Yours sincerely

14 A new land

Vocabulary

Comment adverbials and intensifying adverbs

1 Rewrite the sentences using an adverb from the box.

> absolutely   apparently   fortunately
> incredibly   ~~obviously~~   personally
> to be honest   wisely   undoubtedly

1 It is clear that the cost of living will rise.

Obviously, the cost of living will rise.

2 It is difficult to believe that Adriana got the highest mark in the test.

3 What I think is that young people shouldn't be allowed to drive until the age of 18.

4 People are saying that the new building in town is going to be a sports centre.

5 It is lucky that the weather forecast is good for Kirsty and Dan's wedding day.

6 It's certain that the strike by air traffic controllers will close the airport.

7 Jamie decided not to drive in these icy conditions, which was sensible of him.

8 Melanie was really, really devastated when she found out she'd failed her driving test.

9 I'm not lying – I'm sick of Brooke's behaviour.

provide, offer or *give*

2 Complete the sentences with the correct form of *provide*, *offer* or *give*.

1 Can I .... you a complimentary drink with your meal?

2 As it's a state school, all the exercise books are .... free of charge.

3 Martin always .... to help once most of the work has been done.

4 Rachel .... me so much support when I was ill last year.

5 The travel company .... us the chance to book an extra night.

6 To hire a car, you will need to .... some proof of identity.

7 I .... Julio a lift, but he said he'd rather walk.

8 I bring my own headphones when I travel because the ones the airline .... are poor quality.

Grammar

Emphasis

1 Rewrite the sentences to make them more emphatic using the word or phrase in brackets.

1 I haven't met such rude people before. (Never have …)

Never have I met such rude people.

2 I want to know how many people end up returning to their home country. (What I …)

3 I like Florence but I wish there were fewer tourists. (I do …)

4 My mum wants her children to be happy. (My mum wants all …)

5 We were happiest in Brighton. (The place where we …)

6 The police chief came out to welcome us. (The police chief …)

7 I feel sorry for those who have lost their homes. (It is those)

8 They were so shocked by the news that everyone was silent for several minutes. (The news was so …)

9 I want to go home and get into bed. (The only thing I …)

2 Find and correct the errors in eight of these sentences. The first one has been done for you.

1 I love something about my hometown is that people drive courteously.

Something I love about my hometown is that people drive courteously.

2 Why I asked about the car because I might be interested in buying it.

3 More important than anything is getting the survivors to safety.

4 You could do one thing to help is stack the chairs.

5 Herself the president gave out the awards.

6 What believe I is that everyone has their own unique talents.

7 Best of all is that we have a few extra days off work.

8 Who started all the problems was Tyler.

9 Rarely I have seen so many elephants in one herd.

10 All what I need is enough money to live on.

11 Had I not seen it with my own eyes, I wouldn't have believed it.

Writing Part 1
An essay

1 Read the Part 1 task and then read the students' introductions and answer these questions.

Which student(s):

1 writes too informally?
2 provides a reason not mentioned in the task?
3 states their opinion?
4 provides two reasons?
5 starts with a general topic sentence?

2 Which student's introduction is the most appropriate for this task?

Your class has listened to a radio discussion about the recent trend of moving out of big cities for a life in the countryside. You have made the notes below.

Reasons for moving out of cities:

• Pace of life
• Pollution
• Crime

Some opinions expressed in the discussion

'Many people need to slow down.'
'Health issues are more common in cities.'
'The countryside is a lot safer.'

Write an **essay** discussing **two** of the reasons in your notes for people moving out of big cities. You should **explain why the reasons are important** and **provide reasons** in support of your answer.

You may if you wish make use of the opinions expressed in the discussion, but you should use your own words as far as possible.

Sasha

Apparently, people have now started to move out of cities. This may not be true in all parts of the world but definitely it's happening in richer countries. There has to be a reason for this so I'm going to talk about pollution and crime as I've heard that might be why.

Carlos

Cities in all parts of the world have been growing rapidly for well over a century. However, in recent decades, residents of urban areas in developed countries have started to migrate to more rural areas. This essay will consider two possible reasons: pollution and crime.

Martina

There is a growing trend for people to move out of cities towards rural areas. My own view is that pollution is driving this trend because it is making children ill. Not only that, but the cost of living is rising and people can no longer afford to live in cities.

Use a variety of different phrases to express your opinion throughout your essay and give examples to support your opinion.

Exam advice

3 Read the model essay and highlight all the opinion phrases used.

From the time of the industrial revolution, people have been migrating towards big cities in search of jobs, education and a better way of life. However, in recent decades, there have been signs of a reversal of this trend, with people moving to the countryside. In this essay, I will discuss what I believe are two of the main reasons for this: the pace of life and crime.

I am of the view that it is the desire for a slower pace of life that is the main driver of migration towards village and rural areas. While the fast-paced city lifestyle might suit the young, it is less popular with those raising families and older adults. In my experience, people have more time for each other in the countryside. They are more likely to stop for a chat and to help their neighbours, which, to my mind, raises the overall quality of life.

I would also suggest that high crime rates influence many people's decisions to move out of cities. I am in no doubt that older people, who are more vulnerable to crime, as well as parents seeking to protect their children, see crime as the biggest disadvantage of city life. Both while at home and out and about, there is a lower chance of being a victim of theft or violent crime.

In conclusion, I am convinced that the more relaxed pace of life and safer streets are two reasons why people are choosing to leave over-populated urban areas in favour of more rural places.

---

4 Correct the errors in these opinion sentences.

1 In my opinion, I think that polluted air affects young children the most.
2 I agree with that the countryside is a better place to raise a family.
3 It is clearly that pollution levels are continuing to rise.
4 As far as I concerned, cities are too dangerous for elderly people.
5 Absolutely I am sure that pollution is the main reason for people to leave cities.
6 In my point of view, the fast pace of life causes stress.

Reading and Use of English Part 6

You are going to read four reviews of a book on the history of migration to Australia. Choose from the reviewers A–D. The reviewers may be chosen more than once.

> You might find it useful to use the margin to note down which question each part of the text relates to and whether the views expressed in each text are positive or negative. This will help you to identify similarities and differences between them.
>
> **Exam advice**

The history of migration to Australia

A Torre Machado's comprehensive tome on the history of migration to Australia is surprisingly brief on the country's origins as a British penal colony where prisoners were exiled. This is, in my view, for propaganda purposes, as Machado clearly avoids any criticism of her adopted homeland. Similarly, the writer fails to question the assumption that Australia is among the most receptive to immigration of all the Western nations. It may well be true, but I'd have liked to have seen this investigated further. I found the level of detail on the arrival of the first settlers 80,000 years ago slightly excessive and I skimmed through that section. Though the many pages of documents and pictures could have been an asset, the poor quality of the reproductions didn't do justice to their historical importance.

B Torre Machado's book began with an in-depth account of the first settlers' movements from Africa to Australia via the islands of Maritime Southeast Asia and Papua New Guinea. I was hooked on the book from that fascinating first chapter. I was expecting more coverage of the practice of deportation from Britain to Australia as a punishment for crimes in the 18th and 19th centuries. However, probably in an attempt to differentiate the book from others on the market, Machado seems to have chosen to focus on the lesser-known aspects of the history of migration. Taking us up to the present day, the writer celebrates Australia's openness to immigration, providing evidence that it compares favourably with other developed countries. The book's numerous visuals captivated me. Machado should be congratulated for unearthing such a unique collection of letters, maps, ships logs, photographs and other documents.

C I first picked up Machado's book on migration to Australia because of the infographics on the front cover. Inside, the vast array of photographs of people and artefacts with informative captions kept me enthralled for ages. A lot of ground was covered in a relatively short book. It was a slight shame, though, that more space couldn't be devoted to the most fascinating area of interest: that Australia used to be a giant prison. However, this is one of the few aspects of Australian history that is taught in schools, so Machado obviously felt it was unnecessary. I'd have preferred more on that to the rather tedious coverage of the ancient migrations thousands of years ago. Another issue for me was the notable absence of space given to the experience of present-day migrants. I felt this was done on purpose as without these voices there was nobody to counter Machado's more than dubious claims that Australia has a universally positive attitude towards migration that differentiates it from other developed countries around the world.

D Machado's fascinating book on migration to Australia proves beyond doubt my own personal belief that present-day Australia is one of the few wealthy nations that welcomes migrants with open arms. Machado has been widely criticised for glossing over the penal colony period. Apparently, she wanted to use this book to explore other aspects of the history, which most people are unaware of. Given the current focus on the rights and dignity of indigenous peoples, I loved the detailed commentary on the diversity of the very first arrivals in Australia. As someone who prefers information to be presented visually, I appreciated the work that had gone into accessing a huge number of photographs and documents, such as a list of the rations given to convicts on the ships. In my opinion however, a much better quality of print could have been achieved to make them clearer for the reader.

Which reviewer

has a different opinion from the others on the reason the book doesn't cover the history of deportation as a punishment in much detail? `1` ☐

has a similar view to A on the amount of information provided on the first settlers in Australia? `2` ☐

has a different view from D regarding Australia's current attitude towards migration. `3` ☐

has a similar opinion to A on the visual aspects of the book? `4` ☐

Listening Part 4

> **Exam advice**
>
> Questions in this section often ask how the speakers feel but are unlikely to use the words given in the options. Make sure you know synonyms for a wide range of feelings and remember the feelings might be implied rather than stated directly.

15 You will hear five short extracts in which people are talking about how their way of speaking in a foreign language has changed after moving abroad.

TASK ONE

Choose from the list (A–H) the main reason the speaker gives for how the way they speak has developed.

A length of time in the place they now live
B attachment to their country of origin
C taking time to speak to locals
D attending classes
E fondness for their new country
F watching and listening to the media
G working in their adopted country
H the age at which they moved

Speaker 1 [ ] **1**
Speaker 2 [ ] **2**
Speaker 3 [ ] **3**
Speaker 4 [ ] **4**
Speaker 5 [ ] **5**

TASK TWO

Choose from the list (A–H) how each speaker feels about the way they now speak.

A proud of their achievement
B embarrassed about their poor progress
C surprised about the changes
D determined to do better
E glad that they didn't give up
F happy with their accent
G anxious when speaking to strangers
H unhappy with others' reactions

Speaker 1 [ ] **6**
Speaker 2 [ ] **7**
Speaker 3 [ ] **8**
Speaker 4 [ ] **9**
Speaker 5 [ ] **10**

Reading and Use of English Part 4

> **Exam advice**
>
> For some questions, you might need to change a verb phrase to a noun phrase, for example, which might require the addition of a preposition and a change in sentence pattern. For example, *she intended to* would become *she had the intention of + ing*.

Complete the second sentence so that it has a similar meaning to the first sentence, using the word given. Do not change the word given. You must use between three and six words, including the word given. Here is an example:

Example

0 When people hear someone talk about Italian food, they often think of pizza.
MIND
It is often ....*pizza that comes to mind*.......... when people hear someone talking about Italian food.

1 Photography is not allowed during the performance.
PROHIBITED
Members of the audience .... photographs during the performance.

2 It was wrong of Sue to oppose the donation.
OBJECTED
Sue should .... the donation.

3 Should I be wrong, I'll accept responsibility for it.
MUSIC
I'll .... wrong.

4 David has had flu for the last week.
SUFFERING
David .... flu for the last week.

5 I used to enjoy gardening more than I do nowadays.
PLEASURE
Nowadays, I don't take .... I used to.

6 No-one has ever been that rude to me.
SPOKEN
Never .... rudely.

Workbook answer key with audioscripts Units 1–14

Unit 1 People like us

Grammar

1
1 was growing up
2 were
3 had
4 had always wanted
5 loved
6 got
7 had been spoiling
8 had become
9 were
10 've been trying

2
1 Correct
2 When I was walking down the high street on Saturday, I **had** bumped into a girl I was at school with.
3 Yesterday was a school day so what ~~have you been doing~~ **were you doing** hanging round in the park at 10 in the morning?
4 My brother ~~would used to~~ be a faster runner than me but nowadays I can run much faster than he can.
5 Correct
6 When Marlena finally turned up, we ~~have had~~ been waiting for over an hour.
7 Rafi was an imaginative child; he ~~had been~~ **was** always thinking up stories.
8 I think I'm losing my voice. I ~~talked~~ **have been talking** all day.

3
1 had, was/were
2 fell, had failed
3 would pack/used to pack/packed, went/would go/go/used to go
4 was happening/was barking
5 hadn't been working, joined
6 have been gardening
7 was, had never met
8 managed, headed

Vocabulary

1
| 1 made | 2 give | 3 gave | 4 giving |
| 5 made | 6 making | 7 give | 8 give |

2
1 make an apology; B
2 give (someone) a refund/their money back; F
3 give a lecture; D
4 give (someone) some information/details; A
5 make a phone call; H
6 make a suggestion; G
7 make a comment; C
8 give (someone) instructions; E

Reading and Use of English Part 4

1 is/'s delivered on a weekly basis
2 to increase the length
3 had/'d never paid/hadn't paid a visit to
4 no/little harm in taking (out)/getting
5 don't/do not have as many children
6 to put a stop

Listening Part 4

Task one
1 B   2 D   3 C   4 G   5 E
Task two
6 G   7 B   8 F   9 C   10 E

Track 2

Narrator: You will hear five short extracts in which people are talking about someone they admire. For questions 1–5, choose from the list (A–H) the qualities each speaker believes the person they admire has. For questions 6–10, choose from the list (A–H) what change the speaker made as a result of this person's influence.

1
Woman: My friendship with Amina is a bit unusual as she's a classmate of my older sister. I used to be extremely reserved and had no confidence. Amina and I just clicked and she was such a joy to be around, which is what I really like about her. We've both been into skateboarding since we were young – from long before we met. Amina's introduced me to loads of the people at the skate park who we've been meeting up with and hanging out with. I still have issues with self-esteem, but Amina encourages me to overcome them. We share the dream of opening a skate park together – I'd love to go into business with her one day.

2
Woman: Debi's an old family friend. When the café I owned was doing badly, my parents suggested I approach her. I was a bit apprehensive at first. I felt stupid having borrowed money for the business and my confidence was at rock bottom. Also, she'd always scared me a little. Now though, I'm so glad we met. She looked at all my incomings and outgoings, highlighted the issues and found ways I could fix them. Debi introduced me to a business adviser, who gave me free advice. It was his suggestion to turn the cafe into a 'green' restaurant with vegan food and no waste. Now business is booming, and I no longer owe a cent to anyone.

3
Man: I didn't care about school , I just wanted to have fun. But by my mid 20s I wanted more. I got accepted onto a nursing degree and graduated at the age of 28. It was tough and I have to thank my mentor, Alex, for getting me through it. He's in his 50's and became a nurse when men were a minority in the profession. That never bothered him though. He didn't want to be like everyone else and his friendly manner won people over. He's really supported me in what can be a stressful job, never dismissing me as just some silly kid, just helping me do something worthwhile with my life.

4
Woman: I had it all – I was fit, healthy, had a great social life. Then, a couple of years ago, I had a serious accident. Carley was my occupational therapist. I did basket weaving as part of my therapy to help my injured hand. Personality-wise, we're opposites. Whereas I'm outgoing and sometimes too loud, she always knows her own mind and rarely gets flustered. Plus I love the way she's willing to own up to her own failings. I felt depressed about having no money, but through Carley I became more chilled. I found I have a knack for making things with my hands and thanks to her, I'm still making baskets. I might even sell some online one day.

5
Man: I love talking to my uncle Antonio. Even though I hate football, I used to go and watch it with him just so we could talk. I thought he was the smartest person around. Now I realise he just carries himself well. He has this way of talking that means you always end up agreeing with him. It's amazing.

He's always taken an interest in what I'm doing, even though I tell him to mind his own business. I used to be shy and lack confidence, but he made me believe in myself and follow my dreams. I don't think I would have had the confidence to become a professional pilot if it wasn't for him.

Reading and Use of English Part 8

1 D   2 A   3 B   4 C   5 B   6 A   7 D   8 C   9 B   10 D

Writing Part 1

1
1 No   2 Yes   3 No   4 Yes   5 No

2
1 However/Nevertheless   6 since
2 in this way   7 Secondly
3 Firstly   8 Moreover
4 despite   9 Nevertheless/However/On the other hand
5 On the other hand/However 10 Although

3
1 Yes   2 Yes   3 Yes   4 Yes   5 Yes

Unit 2 More than words

Vocabulary

1
1 got   6 make
2 does   7 do
3 get   8 get
4 do   9 make
5 make   10 doing

2
1 doing   6 get
2 made   7 make
3 made   8 get/do
4 makes   9 making
5 make   10 do

Grammar

1
1 for the purpose of
2 this reason
3 Since
4 Therefore
5 so as
6 in case
7 in order to
8 As a consequence of

2
1 Let's turn the subtitles on **in case** we don't understand everything.
2 We took lots of photos on holiday **so that** we can remember the good times.
3 **As** Leon hasn't spoken French for several years, his French is a bit rusty.
4 Samira lived in Greece as a child, **with the result that** she speaks Greek really well.
5 The lecture was cancelled **due to** the illness of the lecturer/the lecturer being ill.
6 The school reduced the fees **with the intention of** getting more students.

Listening Part 1

1 C   2 B   3 A   4 B   5 C   6 A

Track 3	
Narrator:	You will hear three different extracts. For questions 1-6, choose the answer (A, B or C) that fits best according to what you hear. There are two questions for each extract. Extract 1. You hear two friends discussing a TV documentary about how babies learn to speak.
Woman:	So, what did you think of that programme about babies learning to speak?
Man:	Well, some things really surprised me. I mean I suppose it makes sense that they're born with an innate linguistic capacity—I just hadn't thought of it like that before. What I thought was astonishing was that soon after birth, they're capable of picking up sounds and imitating them whether or not they're from their mother tongue. By a year old, they've kind of homed in on just the language the people around them are speaking. That's fascinating, don't you think?
Woman:	Absolutely. One thing I hadn't been aware of previously was that whatever language they're learning, babies all go through the same process, the same set of milestones, even though as we all know, they all move at their own pace. The more you talk to babies, the quicker they learn, which I'd assumed was the case from being with my sister and her kids. I used to wonder why she kept talking to these tiny babies who couldn't understand her but by the age of one, all of them were stringing words together.
Narrator:	Extract 2. You hear two friends talking about a language speaking test in schools.
Woman:	So, have you seen the new proposals for language teaching in UK secondary schools? I'm amazed that they're doing away with the speaking test. I mean why learn a language if you can't actually use it to have a conversation?
Man:	I'd say the media has twisted this story out of all recognition. Students will still be taught speaking skills but rather than getting an examiner in, at great cost and inconvenience, the teachers can award a grade. It makes more sense in a way, as the teachers know the kids. So, the change is not that major, actually.
Woman:	Well, that does make sense, and the reduced pressure may induce more students to take up a language. It'd be ridiculous though if studying a language weren't mandatory beyond the age of 14, don't you think?
Man:	Mm, that's a tricky one. Research has shown that students simply won't learn a language unless they see the value of it. Now that English is such a widely-used language, convincing children that other languages are important isn't easy.
Woman:	None of that is wrong, but many children probably wouldn't choose to study anything at all, given the choice, so it doesn't justify removing languages from the curriculum.
Narrator:	Extract 3. You hear a man talking to a woman about a text message he has received from his daughter.
Man:	I've just got this text from my daughter, and I have absolutely no idea what it means. I'll have to reply and ask her to write it in proper English. Half of it is in abbreviations- TBH, LMK, G2G and the rest is in these little symbols-emojis, I think they're called. This generation are going to completely destroy the English language.
Woman:	Seriously? You talk as if a language is something static – written in stone. We invented words when we were young, and our parents probably did the same thing. Think of the language writers in the past used – a lot of it is incomprehensible to us now.
Man:	You've got a point I suppose, but it's slightly different, isn't it? I mean, the playwright Shakespeare lived over 400 years ago, so it's logical that we can't always understand him, but my daughter is only 28 years younger than me!
Woman:	Well, yes, but think about why this happens. We used to call a 'pram' a 'perambulator' – cutting five syllables down to one seems reasonable to me. They're just doing the same, but in writing. BRB is three letters, whereas 'be right back' is – let me see – 11 letters.

Reading and Use of English Part 3

1 UNCONVENTIONAL
2 REPETITIVE/REPEATED
3 UNDERESTIMATE/UNDER-ESTIMATE
4 DIFFERENTIATE
5 MISLEADING
6 INDICATION
7 CONTENTMENT
8 AWARENESS

Writing Part 2

2
1 The developer of the app
2 Write, evaluate, suggest
3 To evaluate the user's experiences with the app for Beginners and Advanced learners, and suggest ways to improve it.

3
1 Introduction
2 General evaluation
3 The free app
4 The premium version
5 Recommendations

4
1 attractive, enjoyable, effective
2 outstanding
3 astonished
4 colourful, entertaining
5 reasonable
6 useful, engaging
7 disappointing

Reading and Use of English Part 6

1 B   2 D   3 A   4 C

Unit 3   Mind, body and soul

Vocabulary

1
1 done away with
2 getting into
3 come up
4 comes across as
5 take on
6 rush into
7 put forward
8 catch on

2
1 to catch … with
2 take … time
3 caught … eye
4 make … meet
5 made … point
6 take … as
7 ran … problems

3
1 caught her eye
2 make ends meet
3 ran into problems
4 catch up with
5 make a point of buying
6 can take your time
7 takes things as they come

Grammar

1
1 no   2 none   3 not   4 no   5 Not
6 none   7 not   8 no   9 None   10 no

2
1 It has been **reported** that girls and boys now perform equally well in Maths and Science.
2 Correct
3 Correct
4 Evidence **is** currently being reviewed which suggests that intelligence is inherited from the mother not the father.
5 A child's position in the family **strongly influences** his or her character.
6 Correct
7 The importance of interacting with babies cannot **be** underestimated.
8 Emotional intelligence has **been** shown to be crucial to success at work.
9 Most people **still think/It is generally thought** that the school you go to makes a difference to your educational achievement
10 Tests **have been carried** out to determine the cause of the injury.
11 Errors **can be found/You can find errors** in the test results if you look carefully.
12 Correct

3
1 are judged   6 has been/is shown
2 are given   7 are nurtured
3 know   8 has
4 excel   9 have abandoned
5 are overlooked   10 are used

Listening Part 2

1
1 35%   5 bank transfer
2 music festival   6 video chats
3 visas   7 trust in authority
4 security check   8 primary schools

Track 4

Narrator: You will hear a psychologist called Meera Khan talking about the rise in scamming where people are tricked by others who are trying to make a profit through deception. Complete the sentences with a word or short phrase.

Meera: Psychologists have long been interested in how people get taken in by scams where people try to make money by deceiving others. Approximately 30% of us have been targeted by scammers in the last two years and there's been a growth of 35% in the number of scams being reported during the same period. What's more, at least 10% of people know someone who's lost money to fraud.

A common scam relates to tickets. I recently spoke to a woman, Amy who had bought tickets for a music festival from a website she thought she'd previously used to buy concert tickets. They cost hundreds of dollars, the same price as many sports events. The tickets never materialised. It turned out she'd bought the tickets from a copycat website controlled by criminals.

Many serious cases of fraud are attributed to such fake copycat websites, especially those pretending to be government websites. Driving licenses are a common source of income for criminals, as are passport renewals and travel insurance. I worked on a case where a husband and wife were jailed after making £37 million through online sales for visas which, of course, never existed.

Another type of scam targets jobseekers. An unemployed man called William was offered a CV writing service, which he refused. The same company then told him they'd got him an interview with a top company, but he would have to get a security check at his own expense, which he did. Even after he'd discovered the company was fake, they kept asking him to pay for a training course that never existed.

Shopping online has also been associated with a rise in scams. Experts advise consumers never to pay for goods purchased on the internet via bank transfer. There are several reputable third-party payment providers and credit cards provide a safe option, though do check whether fees apply before making your purchase.

Some upsetting scams are those where people meet through dating websites. Everyone should be vigilant about this happening to family and friends. A preference for voice calls or text conversations rather than video chats is one red flag to watch out for. And 'dates' who ask for money should always be treated with caution.

So which people are most at risk of falling for scams? Well, let's take the fake government websites I mentioned earlier. This scam works best on people who possess a trust in authority, normally considered a positive characteristic. While old and vulnerable people are more likely to come under this category, many younger, tech-savvy individuals have fallen for this scam, and will do so again in the future.

Education is the only way to stop scammers. Some secondary schools are starting to teach children that if something looks too good to be true, it probably is. This is great but starting even earlier, at primary schools, would really ensure a scam-aware society. But for older people, public awareness campaigns on TV, websites and in newspapers would help a lot.

Reading and Use of English Part 2

1 what
2 to
3 on
4 no
5 taken/made
6 so/this/that
7 instead
8 none

Writing Part 1

1
1 Paragraph 3 and the final paragraph.
2 'One could also argue that…', which distances the writer from this opinion.
3 Yes – if celebrities are shown doing things/using products that are inaccessible to some people, it won't be successful.

2
1 But what we disagree on is …
2 strongly influence/deliberately targets
3 namely
4 convince, influence
5 could be encouraged, are seen to do
6 On the one hand/However/Though

3
1 Tax food and drink that are high in fat, salt or sugar
2 Sportsmen and women, film stars and singers
3 Encouraging people to adopt healthy lifestyles
4 Taxing unhealthy food and celebrity endorsement
5 An approach
6 people

Unit 4 Career paths

Vocabulary

1
1 partner with
2 reliance on
3 invest in
4 focus on
5 prevent, from
6 desperate, for
7 conscious of

2
1 fierce
2 specialist
3 vast
4 high
5 extensive
6 powerful
7 unrivalled
8 constant
9 large
10 considerable

3
1 huge/intense
2 excellent
3 excellent/extensive/great
4 great
5 an excellent/a vast
6 great/huge
7 excellent
8 great/heavy/huge/intense
9 huge/great/vast
10 great/huge/large

Grammar

1
3, 4, 6, 8

2
1 possible
2 any chance
3 could well
4 more likely
5 strong likelihood
6 could have
7 bound to
8 every possibility

3
1 Serge is highly unlikely **to** become a doctor.
2 Brooke ~~mustn't~~ **can't/couldn't** have studied enough or she would have passed the exam.
3 We **could well** go out of business if things don't improve.
4 You might ~~easy~~ **easily** have mistaken George for his cousin – they look so alike.
5 Abigail is bound to ~~coming~~ **come** top in the test– she's so smart.
6 Correct
7 One of the possible **reasons** for rising unemployment is lack of consumer confidence.
8 Correct

Listening Part 3

1 C   2 D   3 D   4 B   5 A   6 C

Track 5	
Narrator:	You will hear an interview with a man called Mike Jennings who works as a tea taster and a woman called Lara McDermott who imports tea to the UK. Choose the answer (A, B, C or D) which fits best according to what you hear.
Interviewer:	Today on our series on careers options, we're talking to two people whose career choices are definitely my cup of tea! Mike Jennings is a tea taster and Lara McDermott imports tea to the UK. Welcome, both of you. So, Mike, can you tell us how you got into tea tasting?
Man:	Well, actually, it was something I stumbled into. I'd graduated from university with a Science degree but had gone out to Sri Lanka to teach English, while deciding what to do with my life. One day, a friend of mine fancied visiting a tea factory and I went along for the ride, but it wasn't until I got there that I realised how special that visit would be for me. I suppose you would call it a 'eureka' moment. I got chatting to a factory manager and heard all about the fascinating process of planting, harvesting, drying and of course tasting and blending. And that was it – I'd found my career!

Interviewer:	So, what would you say are the most important qualities for a tea taster?
Man:	Erm, there's no fixed route into being a taster. My colleagues have all done different degrees. A background in science, while useful, isn't a necessity though much of the time you're working in a laboratory-like environment. You do need to be aware of climatic conditions, though, and how they affect soil and how water temperature affects the taste of the tea. Yes, I'd say the main thing is to have a good palette and an active olfactory nerve, since taste and smell are so closely related. Although you become more aware of your senses as you train, if those essentials are missing, you'll never make it.
Interviewer:	Just out of curiosity, I've always wondered why tea tasters slurp their tea in that noisy way. It's not considered very polite normally so is there a reason for it?
Man:	Yes, of course. Some people think we don't care about politeness because we're behind closed doors. But there is a reason for it. When we conduct a tasting, we drink from a large spoon to ensure that the tea itself has plenty of oxygen. Putting tea in a cup would prevent that. We then need to ensure that as we're drinking the tea, it passes over all the taste receptors in the tongue so we get an even taste profile of the tea. Hence, the slurp. It's how it's been done for centuries and there is still no better way of doing it.
Interviewer:	Ah, that makes sense. Let's bring Lara in here. Lara, you import tea to the UK. How do you tell if a tea is top quality or not?
Woman:	It's actually fairly easy. The best tea is not processed by machine, using the CTC (cut, tear, curl) method. Its texture isn't crumbly and it doesn't contain lots of stalks. The other method, known as the orthodox method, minimises the handling of the tea leaves and preserves the delicate flavours. It can be hard to find tea using this method in the UK as we don't import much in. Most of the tea we drink is produced with the CTC method.
Interviewer:	That's interesting. Do people in the UK have strong views about how tea should be drunk?
Woman:	Definitely! If you ask ten people how they like their tea, you'll get ten different answers. People mention the brands they like and how long they brew it for. In the UK, 98% of people drink traditional black tea with milk. But there has been a slight shift in recent years. Green and herbal teas are growing in popularity, especially among the twenty somethings, so are iced teas, which were unheard of here until relatively recently. Older people are most attached to the traditional black tea with milk and maybe sugar.
Interviewer:	So, Mike and Lara, the question lots of our listeners want me to ask you is which is more popular in the UK, tea or coffee?
Man:	Tea, for sure!
Woman:	Definitely, tea!
Interviewer:	Why do you think that is?
Man:	Well, I should start by saying, coffee is catching up. I read recently that the number of cups of coffee drunk per day rose from 70 million to 95 million between 2008 and 2018. That's obviously due to the explosion in the number of coffee shops and the cool image of coffee. But tea is deeply embedded in our way of life. Whenever someone has a problem, the solution is a cup of tea. Coffee will never have that comfort factor, at least not here.
Woman:	I tend to agree with Mike about British people seeing coffee as being cooler and more sophisticated, but I'd say it's the lower level of caffeine in tea that will mean its popularity will endure. I mean, personally, I can only drink one or two coffees a day but can drink five or six teas easily.

Reading and Use of English Part 8

1 C   2 A   3 D   4 D   5 A   6 B   7 D   8 B   9 C   10 C

Writing part 2

1
1 F (a friend of a friend)
2 T
3 F (Sarah)
4 F (informal but not slang)
5 F (she is going for an interview at your company)

2
1 position	5 organisational
2 short-listed	6 mission statement
3 collaboratively	7 policy
4 team player	8 workplace

3
1 Try showing > Try to show
2 Correct
3 I suggest you finding > I suggest you find
4 Correct
5 that's worth mention! > That's worth mentioning!/That's worth a mention!
6 I'd advice you to dress > I'd advise you to dress
7 Avoid to wear > Avoid wearing

Unit 5 Events to remember

Vocabulary

1
1 back	2 leg	3 fingers
4 eye	5 arm	6 back

2
1 pick	2 jumping	3 tied	4 lightly
5 mend	6 up	7 settle	8 wonder

Grammar

1
1 getting	2 to stick	3 to have	4 leaving	5 to attend
6 feeling	7 making	8 growing	9 to keep	10 to have

2
1 Would you mind ~~to drop~~ **dropping** me off at the hospital on your way home?
2 Correct
3 Annie pretended ~~having~~ **to have** a degree from a top university in order to get the job.
4 I expect ~~getting~~ **to get** good grades in English and French but not in Maths.
5 Javier admitted ~~be~~ **being** a little bit jealous of his brother's success.
6 I refuse ~~apologising~~ **to apologise** for telling the truth.
7 Correct
8 You're such a good speaker. Would you consider ~~join~~ **joining** the debating society?
9 Correct
10 Correct

Listening Part 1

1 B **2** C **3** B **4** A **5** A **6** C

Reading and Use of English Part 4

1 despite Richard's insistence on planning
2 do our utmost/take the utmost care/make the utmost effort to prevent
3 be cancelled at short notice
4 in keeping her word
5 by far the funniest/far funnier than any other
6 never worked round/around the clock

Reading and Use of English Part 7

1 D **2** E **3** C **4** G **5** A **6** F

Writing

1
1 The principal objective
2 At present
3 What's more
4 provide an opportunity
5 Furthermore
6 a real need
7 I propose
8 must take advantage of

2

1 profile	**5** formal
2 provides	**6** put forward
3 fitting	**7** cover
4 mingle	**8** enables

3
Suggested answers:
1 Introduction
2 The venue / The location
3 Activities
4 Publicity / Marketing
5 Conclusion / Final recommendations

Unit 6 Creative pursuits

Grammar

1

1 one	**2** so	**3** which	**4** so	**5** could
6 This	**7** others	**8** both	**9** another	**10** some

2
1 Maddy would have been a ballerina if she had had the opportunity ~~to be a ballet dancer~~.
2 My uncle promised to take me to the Liverpool game but he didn't ~~take me to the Liverpool game~~.
3 I was sure we would win the match but the rest of the team weren't ~~sure we would win the match~~.
4 There are no art galleries in my town but I wish there were ~~some art galleries in my town~~.
5 I've never been to see an opera but I'd like to ~~go and see an opera~~.
6 There was an amazing craft market in the square last Sunday and next Sunday there will be another ~~amazing craft market in the square~~.
7 Noor isn't happy with her music classes but her brother is ~~happy with his music classes~~.
8 Miss Nicholls asked Isaac to help clear up the mess but he refused ~~to help clear up the mess~~.

3

1 these/them	**6** whose
2 Another	**7** mine
3 both	**8** had
4 one	**9** Others/Some/They
5 so	**10** them

Vocabulary

1
1 fair
2 high
3 an endless
4 terrible
5 huge
6 satisfactory
7 valuable
8 wide
9 heavy
10 terrible

2
1 correct
2 great, good, tremendous, huge
3 steady, remarkable, considerable
4 correct
5 correct
6 large, good, huge
7 terrible
8 great
9 correct
10 small, modest, limited, tiny

Reading and Use of English Part 5

1 C 2 D 3 B 4 C 5 A 6 B

Listening Part 2

1 the Arabian gulf 2 fuel 3 iceberg 4 eye contact
5 trunk 6 laws 7 dance 8 Welsh

Track 7	
Narrator:	You will hear a university lecturer called Jenny Warren giving a talk about culture. Complete the sentences with a word or short phrase.
Jenny:	Culture is one of the most complex and hard to pin down concepts, because it is concerned with almost every aspect of human experience.
	Consider food, for example. Everyone knows there are a huge variety of cuisines out there but how did they start? Obviously, island nations like the Maldives tend to eat more fish and the type of crops which grow in the local climate and soil dictate the basis of many dishes, such as olives in the Mediterranean and in the Arabian gulf where it is difficult to grow crops like apples, strawberries or grapes, dates are often used.
	Culinary methods too are influenced by culture and geography. In parts of China, the scarcity of fuel meant that food had to be cut finely and fried quickly. The Maori of New Zealand often boil food using hot springs which have unique geothermal properties. Food is laid on rocks and covered with flax leaves or more recently, cloth sacks.
	There is no single agreed definition of culture. Different models exist that provide a comparison of culture with an actual thing. Some people compare culture to an onion or a rulebook in invisible ink, but the model I find easiest to comprehend is the analogy of culture as an iceberg.
	In this model we have seen and unseen cultural artefacts i.e. clothes, food, festivals – about 10% of what we call culture is visible – but there are also many things that are more difficult to observe – like eye contact – things where there are rules but these aren't easily understood.
	Another favoured analogy is the tree. The leaves represent the observable aspects while the trunk is norms and values and the roots are the origins of the culture, myths, legends, stories – things that can't be changed and even members may be unaware of.
	A newer model invented by Jürgen Bolton is based on a sand dune. At the sediment level are laws – things an individual MUST adhere to. The sand in the middle represents aspects which should be followed and at the top are the shifting sands, which symbolise the parts of culture that are open to change.

Of course, there are many traditions unique to a particular culture. In recent years, organisations, such as UNESCO have tried to protect the cultural heritage of minority groups in society by recognising different practices and art forms. For example, Hula, the dance form developed by the Polynesians who originally settled in Hawaii, should be recognised and appreciated as a symbol of Hawaiian identity.

The UK is considered multicultural for many reasons. One of these is the fact that the UK is made up of four different countries: England, Scotland, Wales and Northern Ireland, each with its own unique traditions and linguistic history. Concerted efforts have been made to preserve these cultures. As an example, unlike English which is the predominant language spoken throughout the UK, Welsh was on the verge of extinction. It is now taught in many more schools in Wales and is an option for anyone interacting with any government website in the UK.

Writing Part 2

1
1 reality 2 bunch 3 basket 4 end
5 plan 6 household 7 home 8 recipe

2
1 (surprisingly) addictive
2 (really) relatable
3 stunning, imaginative, (technically) brilliant
4 disappointing
5 scorching
6 famous, typical

3
1 Why I like it is …
2 I've been glued to it
3 find yourself rooting for them
4 For me, the highlight of the season was
5 My absolute favourite is
6 I highly recommend

Unit 7 In your free time

Vocabulary

1
1 behalf of
2 keeping with
3 aid of
4 exchange for
5 place of
6 account of
7 far from
8 means of
9 regard to

2
1 costs, fortune
2 pay by card
3 take out, loan
4 sell himself
5 earn, living
6 make, buck
7 rent, hire
8 lend, pay, back
9 money, burn
10 afford, raise

3
1 f 2 d 3 h 4 b 5 g 6 i 7 c 8 a 9 e

4
1 paid peanuts
2 spending money like water
3 holds the purse strings
4 pay through the nose
5 rolling in money
6 Money doesn't grow on trees
7 put your money where your mouth is
8 pay my own way

Grammar

1
1 (which/that) (no commas)
2 whose (no commas)
3 *Mean Girls*, which was released in 2004, was a typical American high school movie.
4 which/that (no commas)
5 where (no commas)
6 My elder brother, who was always fixing things around the house, has just qualified as an engineer.
7 who/that (no commas)
8 Parkour, which is similar to free running, can be quite dangerous.
9 (which/that) (no commas)
10 Harlan Coben, whose books I love, is an American novelist.

2
1 Josefina ran down the road, calling her brother's name.
2 Built in 1595, this is the oldest house in the village.
3 Having studied French at university, Evie was able to understand the film.
4 Made by hand, this lace is really beautiful.
5 The director made a speech thanking everyone for their help.
6 Having passed grade 6 piano, Alvin moved to the grade 7 class.
7 Drunk in small quantities, coffee is good for you.
8 Looking at me suspiciously, Maurice handed me the money.

3
1 Turn right at the Beacon Centre, ~~which is~~ the building next to the school.
2 Jessica, ~~who is~~ the girl I told you about, is standing over there.
3 Freedom, ~~which is~~ the greatest gift of all, is often taken for granted.
4 The O'Connor twins, ~~who are~~ well-known ice-skaters, used to live next door to us.
5 Rounders, ~~which is~~ a baseball-like sport, is very popular in England.
6 My students, ~~who were~~ all Japanese, were amazing at origami.

Reading and Use of English Part 1

1 C 2 A 3 B 4 B 5 D 6 C 7 A 8 D

Listening Part 4

Task One
1 F	distractors D, G
2 A	distractors H, B
3 C	distractors A, E, G
4 B	distractors G, H
5 H	distractors G, A

Task Two
6 H	distractors A, E
7 C	distractor D
8 G	distractor C
9 E	distractor D
10 F	distractor B

Track 8

Narrator: You will hear five short extracts in which people are talking about taking part in different events for charity. For questions 1–5, choose from the list (A–H) the main reason each speaker gives for taking part in the event. For questions 6–10, choose from the list (A–H) the way the speaker feels about their event now.

1
Woman: Although I hate the idea of being in the public eye, the fact that there are kids in our town who regularly go without meals meant I had to do something. People just don't know about this stuff and I thought the sight of a 60-year-old woman raising money for charity by abseiling down a 200-metre-high tower would make people sit up and take notice. It was good to finally do it, as we'd had to postpone the event three times due to the weather, which was annoying, but I'm not proud of the way I screamed 'Help me!' all the way down.

2
Woman: I've always loved swimming and I'd achieved several swimming-related ambitions, but I'd never used my love for the sport to help anyone else until I took part in the 10k 'swimathon' in aid of a local rehabilitation centre. A few years ago, I had an accident and spent months recuperating at the centre. It's a great facility with the latest equipment but it relies on donations to run. I really wanted to express my gratitude by doing the swim. It went well and I raised so much that I've now decided to attempt to swim the English Channel. It'll be the hardest – but most thrilling – thing I'll have ever done. Bring it on!

3
Man: I'm terrified of heights so I can't abseil or skydive, so, along with my friend Dan, I organised a sponsored 'gameathon', where we played online games for 12 hours straight. The proceeds went to Age Awareness, a charity close to me as they helped my grandma in her final years. I figured that if others saw you didn't need extreme levels of fitness or courage to help a charity, they'd do the same. I thought it would be exciting to have guilt-free gaming for a whole day, but after enduring a whole day looking at the screen, it's given me a new perspective. I now limit my screen-time and I'm delighted I made this change.

4
Man: I completed a charity skydive a few months ago and, to be honest, I'm just glad to be here to tell the tale. It was petrifying. It was a tandem jump with an instructor from 3,600 metres. We landed, but afterwards the instructor told me the main chute had failed. We'd had to rely on the back-up! My heartrate took hours to return to normal afterwards! It's not like I'd always dreamed of doing something like that, but our local children's hospital needs a new MRI scanner and they'll need 100,000 to cover that. Hopefully I've helped them reach that target.

5
Woman: It was great to raise money for a new local charity but I'd actually signed up to see if I could run a half-marathon. I'd hated sport as a child, but as an adult I run regularly just for fitness and I wondered if I could run that far. In preparation, I gradually ran further and further, but I didn't do 21k, the distance of a half-marathon, before the day. I assumed that the adrenaline would get me through. It didn't. I'm OK with that. I'll try again next year. What got me down though was the negative posts on social media. I thought people would be proud of me. After all, at least I tried!

Writing

1
C, E, B, A, D

2
1 Why don't you
2 could
3 shouldn't
4 If I were you
5 I'd

3
1 huge issue
2 house shares/share a flat
3 hold you back
4 expand your horizons
5 bonding experience
6 start a new venture/give it a go
7 be in the same boat
8 like-minded people

Model answer

A Secondly, I doubt finding accommodation will be a huge issue, either. **(1)** *How about/Why don't you* find out if there's anyone you could share a flat with? If not, most estate agents arrange house shares for young people, which could also be a way to make new friends. You **(2)** *may/could* also ask your HR department if they're able to help.

B Since you're not leaving your company, I'm sure there will be plenty of opportunities to meet up with the colleagues you work with now. They might even get the chance to relocate later on as your boss might decide to move more employees once the new branch is settled there. In any case, you definitely **(3)** *couldn't/shouldn't* let this hold you back.

C It was great to hear from you. How exciting to get the opportunity to move to another town! That's amazing!

D So, all in all, it sounds like a marvellous chance to expand your horizons. Starting a new venture together is sure to be a bonding experience and should be good for your CV too. **(4)** *If I were you/If I'm you*, I'd definitely give it a go.

E It's natural to have a few concerns about such a big chance but in my opinion, there's no need to worry too much about it. First, I assume lots of your colleagues will be going too so I don't think meeting people will be a problem. Everyone will be in the same boat, so at least at first, you can all do stuff together in the evenings. **(5)** *I'll/I'd* advise you to join a gym as you'll meet plenty of like-minded people there.

Unit 8 Sound and vision

Grammar

1
2 Jim said (that) he hadn't gone to university at all.
3 Sonia said (that) was what she was thinking of doing.
4 Jim said (that) he would highly recommend it.
5 Sonia said (that) she would start earning money straight away.
6 Jim asked whether Sonia had considered the possibility of doing her apprenticeship there.
7 Sonia asked Jim whether he knew when the closing date for applications was.
8 Jim said (that) it was the following Friday.
9 Sonia said she'd been hoping (that) Jim/he would say that.

2
2 Becky asked Arturo how long he **had** been living **there**.
3 Charlotte told me that she **hadn't enjoyed** the film because she had seen it before.
4 Charlie wanted to know whether I **had** ever appeared on TV.
5 Correct
6 Tim told me that **he** was still waiting to hear if **he had** got the job at the newspaper.
7 Connie said that her mum **hadn't** watched the news **the previous day**.
8 Correct
9 David asked me why **I was** staring at him.

3
2 My school **arranged for me** to do work experience at an advertising agency.
3 The law **requires you/people/us** to wear a seatbelt, even in the back seat.
4 Luckily, my best friend reminded **me** to give in my assignment before the deadline.
5 Correct
6 Correct
7 You should **admit to your parents** what you did.
8 Correct
9 Correct
10 Our teacher has just informed **us** about the test next week.
11 Amalie refused to help **me** with the project.

Vocabulary

1
2 tell anyone
3 discuss the questions
4 speak clearly/talk
5 mention my name
6 talking nonsense
7 'm telling the truth
8 speaks her mind
9 say nothing
10 express my thanks
11 to comment on the fact

2
1 unpopular
2 inexperienced
3 illegal
4 dissatisfied
5 irrelevant
6 uncertain
7 imperfect
8 inefficient

3
1 disapprove
2 underestimated
3 reconstruct
4 misunderstood
5 relocate
6 interacting

4
2 a misunderstanding
3 reconstruction
4 illegal
5 inexperienced
6 non-fiction

5
1 approval
2 imperfections
3 relevance
4 dissatisfaction
5 unpopularity
6 co-pilot
7 illegality

Reading and use of English Part 3

1 INNOVATIVE
2 ACCOMPLISHMENT
3 CAPABILITY
4 DISTRIBUTION
5 CONSUMPTION
6 UNDENIABLE
7 INNACURATELY
8 INFLUENTIAL

Listening Part 3

1 C   2 A   3 C   4 D   5 B   6 A

Track 9

Narrator: You will hear an interview in which two foreign correspondents called Mark Shelby and Carol Bentall are talking about their work. For questions 1-6, choose the answer (A, B, C or D) which fits best according to what you hear.

Interviewer: Today we're talking to two people who've worked as foreign correspondents, Mark Shelby and Carol Bentall. Welcome, both of you. Let's start with you, Mark. As we know, foreign correspondents are news reporters based in another country. Can you tell us what it takes to do the job you've been doing for the last 15 years?

Mark: Mm, where do I start? It's certainly a job that appeals to the curious, those who want to know all the ins and outs of a situation, and it helps if you're the determined sort of person who won't give up on a story till it's in the bag. But something that's vital, and not always apparent from a person's CV, is the ability to find a fresh angle. To look for stories in the least obvious places, to not just talk to the most obvious people. That talent to notice aspects of a story ignored by everyone else is crucial. Even more than writing skills, which believe it or not, some reporters don't have at all, at least not to the level you'd expect.

Interviewer: And what would you say is the most challenging part of the job?

Mark: Many would say the danger. It's scary sometimes, especially if you're caught up in a conflict miles from home. But that's often worse for the family, who may not have heard from you for weeks, than it is for the correspondent. When you're doing the job, you're caught up in the day-to-day, meeting people, learning about the country, making contacts. In fact, that's when it can seem at its toughest because it's hard to know who to trust at times. Not everyone's truth is the same and it's difficult to build the strong relationships you need when you're living out of a suitcase, moving from one hotel room to another.

Interviewer: Let's bring in Carol here, too. You've been a reporter all over the world for almost 30 years. Can you tell us how things have changed in that time?

Carol: Technology is the big thing, and not every correspondent has enjoyed getting to grips with it. Some of the old guard miss phoning in their report to their editor in London, but I prefer being able to file things on the go – it gives me more control of the story. That said, there's nothing more infuriating than finding yourself somewhere with no 4G coverage. Deadlines are everything and if you can't get your story in on time, you may lose out to a rival. It's why we live in constant fear of breaking our phones.

Interviewer: Mark, what's your view on how the internet has changed the job?

Mark: The answer to that is not as simple as you might expect. Doing our research into the background of a conflict is a lot less effort, but it also means information about us is available, which doesn't necessarily work in our favour. Once something is out there, it's out there. One comment you made years ago could mean someone rejecting all your requests for an interview.

Interviewer: Can you share a story about a memorable moment in your career, Carol?

Carol: Well, yes, there had been a military coup in the country where I was based. The President was in hiding but we'd heard on the grapevine that he was going to come out to make a statement. My source had told me he'd emerge from the bunker under the presidential palace. Only our news organisation had this tip-off and my colleague and I were feeling pretty full of ourselves, confident we were about to get an exclusive story. After many hours camped out in the darkness, we heard he'd appeared somewhere else in the city and another reporter got the scoop. Our informant had meant well so there were no hard feelings. These things happen.

Interviewer: So, can you both offer some advice to young people wanting to follow the same career path?

Carol: Always follow your conscience. You will face moral dilemmas, like knowing a story will enhance your reputation and make you well known, but may put someone else in peril. Learn a few words of many languages because it shows respect and can help you get the story.

Mark: I agree. As a graduate in Arabic and French, I'd suggest an in-depth knowledge of one or two languages will give you a step up. But definitely keep your integrity, not just because it's the right thing to do but because it will work in your favour in the long run.

Writing Part 2

1
1 F (it could be for your peers)
2 F (you should avoid writing a list)
3 T
4 T
5 F (a proposal should be organised into headed sections)
6 T

2
1 Yes 2 Yes 3 Yes

3

Positive	Negative
state-of the art	dated
superior	amateur
exceptional	cluttered
ninimalist	drab
user-friendly	time-consuming
distinctive	saturated
interactive	
innovative	

4
1 will 2 needs 3 would 4 should 5 can 6 could

Unit 9 Invention and innovation

Grammar

1
1 is to be taken over
2 will have been issued/are to be issued
3 will be driving
4 is to address/will be addressing
5 will be joining
6 will have been travelling/will have travelled
7 will be working
8 is to be
9 will be climbing

2
2 My cousin and I never really liked each ~~another~~ **other**, but we get on OK nowadays.
3 Correct
4 I'm going to knit **a jumper for my sister's new baby**.
5 Anouk frequently sends **text messages to her colleagues**/**her colleagues text messages**.
6 My neighbour and I help one ~~other~~ **another**/~~one~~ **each other** when we can.
7 Correct
8 John walked along the office corridor muttering to ~~hisself~~ **himself**.
9 I think you owe ~~to~~ me an explanation for borrowing my car without asking.

Vocabulary

1
1 make
2 lose
3 taken
4 dream up
5 undergone
6 made
7 exercise

2
1 sign in
2 run out
3 scroll through
4 locked out
5 popping up
6 hack into
7 shut down

3
1 d 2 h 3 e 4 i 5 g 6 a 7 b 8 f 9 c

4
1 event
2 programme
3 actions
4 activities
5 event
6 programme
7 activity
8 action

Listening Part 1

1 C 2 A 3 B 4 C 5 B 6 C

Track 10	
Narrator:	You will hear three different extracts. Choose the answer (A, B or C) which fits best according to what you hear. There are two questions for each extract. Extract 1. You hear two friends talking about building a drone.
Boy:	So, what are we trying to prove with this drone?
Girl:	You mean, apart from that we're geniuses? We're showing that the lift generated by the propellers must be greater than or equal to how heavy the drone is for it to stay in the air or fly forward. We could also make it easier to steer the drone by making the propellers spin at different speeds but I'm not sure we could pull that off.
Boy:	Maybe not, but in any case, I don't think putting the drone together will be the hardest part. I have my doubts whether all that stuff we'll need is available locally. Those mini propellers, for example, I've never seen them before.
Girl:	We'll get those online and I'm sure my dad's got a battery pack we can use. We'll build it at school so we can use the glue gun. As you know, we have to keep recording all the data but that'll need high levels of precision. It says to use jewellery scales but I don't think we can get those.
Boy:	Mm, it also mentions kitchen scales, which we do have but I wouldn't have thought they'd be sensitive enough. Anyway, we'll check with Mr Rasheed.
Narrator:	Extract 2. You hear two friends discussing jackets that use smart technology.
Woman:	Have you seen Alexi's new heated jacket?
Man:	Yeah, I doubt whether that kind of jacket's going to catch on here, where it never goes below 10 degrees, but in his country, it gets to minus 20, so you'd assume they'd be popular there.
Woman:	Yeah, you would but I've heard the cost is one reason they're not that popular, and it's yet another battery to keep charged.
Man:	Makes sense. They sound a bit risky to me, especially if you fell into a river or something. You'd get electrocuted, surely.
Woman:	Possibly, but the wires are separated by a waterproof layer, so you should be fine, though the battery probably wouldn't. It says it's designed to stop you getting too hot, but I'd worry about that in this country. What I'd like is an air-conditioned jacket. Is that a thing?
Man:	Apparently, so. I've seen them on TV. The air comes into the coat and it puffs up with cooling air. Not very flattering, admittedly, and they can be a bit bulky, but I suppose that's better than being stuck working in a tunnel or underground on a hot day. That's what they were originally meant for, and compared to using a normal air conditioner, they don't need nearly as much electricity.

Narrator:	Extract 3. You hear a man and woman discussing a science programme they watched on TV.
Woman:	Did you watch the Science Today programme last night?
Man:	About the helium balloons being used to provide remote areas with the internet? Apparently, they create an aerial network up there at the edge of space, making it possible to get online in places that were previously inaccessible. I It was just amazing!
Woman:	I was so excited for the entire first half of the story, but then they got into the whole thing about affordability and import taxes and all the difficulties they've had getting it off the ground. It could change the world – help people do business, get an education, save lives even. It would be a shame if after all they've done and all the funding they've raised, it didn't go anywhere.
Man:	I know. The second part of the programme was interesting too, about other ways of supporting people in remote areas with technology, such as recycling smart phones. It was also amazing how they're using translation apps to overcome the lack of information online once people have access. Who knew that unless you know English, there's so little information you can access on the web? It was such a simple solution too, so I was taken aback that it hadn't been done before.

Reading and Use of English Part 7

1 E 2 G 3 D 4 B 5 A 6 F

Writing Part 1

2
Work experience

3
1 required
2 field
3 industrial
4 gain
5 decisions
6 aside
7 backgrounds
8 running
9 genuine
10 opportunities

4
1 appropriate
2 encourage
3 appreciate
4 alter
5 convince
6 launch

Unit 10 Learning for life

Grammar

1
2 I could ~~order~~ **have ordered** the stationery for you if you had let me/you let me.
3 Correct
4 If we hadn't decided to go to the same university, we might never **have** met.
5 It was difficult but in the end I ~~could~~ **was able to**/**managed to** pass the exam.
6 Jack ~~can~~ **must** have lost the office key. He was the last one to have it.
7 I must ~~have attended~~ **attend** today's lecture. I've missed three already.
8 Hopefully Roshani ~~can~~ **will be** able to retrieve your data for you.

2
2 I couldn't understand my Maths teacher.
3 It must have been Abdul.
4 students had to pay their fees
5 managed/was able to get hold of
6 might have come to the party
7 pupils weren't allowed to talk/couldn't talk while the teacher was talking.

Vocabulary

1
2 possibility
3 chance
4 opportunity
5 opportunity
6 chance

7 occasion
8 chance

2
2 on the off
3 rule out
4 given the
5 on one

6 arises
7 a distinct
8 welcome the
9 an equal

Listening Part 2

1 (international) scholarship (programme)
2 castle
3 welcoming
4 heaters
5 (class) comedian
6 (cross-country) running
7 (fabulous) (afternoon) tea
8 distractions

Track 11

Narrator: You will hear a lecture in which a man called Ajay Fernandez has been asked to talk about his time at a boarding school in Scotland. Complete the sentences with a word or short phrase.

Ajay: Hello. My name is Ajay Fernandez and thank for you for inviting me to talk about my boarding school experience. I attended an all-boys boarding school in the Scottish Highlands called St Stephen's. My parents wanted me to attend the school for a number of reasons.

It had an excellent academic reputation, the sports facilities were second to none and the international scholarship programme meant that it is affordable for gifted students from other countries. My family comes from the Andaman Islands in the Indian Ocean and isn't particularly wealthy, so that final point was the deciding factor for my parents.

After my journey there, I remember my first impression of the school. As I approached it I saw a stately home and I was hoping it would be St Stephen's. But then arriving at last at a castle-like building, I was certainly thrilled that this was going to be my home. It was before the internet, and I'd never seen a picture of it. In my head, I'd imagined it as a bigger version of my village school.

We were met by the headmaster, Mr. McEwan. I'd been nervous about the strict character I'd expected to meet, but the man welcoming us to the school was totally unlike this. Such welcoming characters hadn't featured in my educational experience before as I'd experienced headmasters as stern and aloof.

We were then shown to the dormitory where we were to sleep. This was closer to my expectations – a large room with eight neatly made beds in two rows, each with a chest of drawers next to it. I was relieved to see several heaters mounted on the walls. There were views of the wild and menacing sea from the open windows.

I soon made friends with the other boys in my class. Ahmed was a serious and helpful chap I soon got close to. Donny and Mike were sporty like me, but it was Gerry, who became my best friend. We were inseparable and his role as the class comedian meant we played so many pranks on our classmates and teachers.

There was a massive focus on sports at the school. Rugby and football were the key sports and, all of us being extremely competitive, we all tried to get into the school teams. There were some sports I found unappealing – cross-country running and hockey stand out, the former being an activity I detest even now.

One thing I absolutely loved was travelling to other schools to play matches. We'd miss afternoon lessons, and sing and muck about all the way. The rivalry between teams, though strong, was good-natured enough and we'd always get a fabulous afternoon tea. As a greedy kid, this was the highlight for me, though missing the evening study session came a close second.

I did better academically at St Stephen's than I might have done elsewhere. The strict rules, structured days and plentiful exercise probably contributed but what made me really apply myself was that there were so few distractions. It meant I spent more time reading, a pastime I still love to this day.

Reading and Use of English Part 1

1 C **2** C **3** A **4** B **5** B **6** D **7** A **8** D

Reading and Use of English Part 8

1 C **2** A **3** B **4** D **5** A **6** C **7** D **8** B **9** A **10** C

Writing Part 2

1
1 T
2 T
3 F (At least one more heading is needed. Following the points in the question is often a good way to organise the report.)
4 F (The writer has said what she enjoyed but not what she found beneficial. She has mentioned negative aspects but not made recommendations.)
5 F (Some parts are not relevant, e.g., Molly lived nearby, an old lady told the instructor off)
6 F (It is too informal in places e.g., a good laugh, my mates)
7 F (There are a few complex structures, such as a relative clause but no passives, for example. Vocabulary is quite basic.)

2
1 B **2** C **3** G **4** A **5** F **6** E **7** D

3
1 my own age
2 residential
3 designated
4 tuition
5 nature

6 choice
7 unique
8 self-catering
9 dietary
10 maintenance

4
1 was taught by
2 were offered   was given
3 should be placed   could be spent

Unit 11 Globetrotters

Vocabulary

1

1 e **2** f **3** a **4** h **5** c **6** g **7** b **8** d

2

2 The whole point of choosing

3 rough it

4 out in the open

5 keep his cool

6 gets sick and tired of

7 disappeared without a trace

8 to be kept waiting/being kept waiting

3

at	in	on
a party work	Asia a queue the surroundings	an island the moon the outskirts the phone

4

1 in **2** on **3** in **4** in **5** on **6** at **7** on

8 At **9** at **10** in **11** In **12** in **13** on

Grammar

1

2 'd be lying

3 get

4 's

5 Both (wouldn't have left – he has already left; wouldn't be leaving – he is about to leave)

6 Both (would choose – it is still possible but unlikely; would have chosen – she didn't choose it)

7 'm

8 're

9 Both (I wouldn't be – I'm out of breath now; wouldn't have been – I was out of breath in the past.)

10 's

11 would

2

2 hadn't eaten

3 knew/had known

4 hadn't spent

5 would improve

6 spoke/could speak

7 had booked

8 didn't live

9 would stop

Reading and Use of English Part 2

1 neither

2 being

3 it

4 not

5 makes

6 in

7 account

8 is

Listening Part 1

1 A **2** C **3** C **4** A **5** A **6** B

Track 12

Narrator: You will hear three different extracts. Choose the answer (A, B or C) which fits best according to what you hear. There are two questions for each extract.
Extract 1. You hear a husband and wife comparing holiday resorts.

Man: So, what do you think of this resort? It's nice, isn't it?

Woman: Mm, yes. I mean, It's got a lot going for it. It was easy to get here, it's got a great pool and loads of sunbeds and the food in the restaurant is amazing, the best I've ever had and the waiters were really on the ball. In fact, it really feels like everyone working here goes out of their way to help you. Having said that, I really don't feel comfortable here. Wherever you go, you can hear a pin drop and I'd much prefer to be closer to the beach.

Man: I agree. Where we stayed last summer, everything was on our doorstep. The beach, shops, restaurants, everything, and I know you didn't like the food, but I'm not as fussed about that as you are, and it was great to have the choice to be able to eat what you wanted whenever you liked. Yes, that resort wasn't all-inclusive, but the money we're spending on taxis here means it was probably more economical. Also, do you remember that great boat trip we had? All because we struck up a conversation with the captain. Those chance encounters just don't happen here.

Narrator: Extract 2. You hear a man and a woman talking about occasions they went travelling.

Man: Where did you go on holiday?

Woman: Oh, we went travelling in Thailand.

Man: Haven't they just had monsoon season?

Woman: Yes, and even though we avoided the worst of it, it wasn't ideal. As a result, we spent more time in hostels than we would have wanted. Still, we passed the time swapping stories with the other guests and made some great connections along the way. Sometimes a five-star hotel looked appealing, but we'd have missed out on the social aspect if we'd opted for that.

Man: That's not always what you want from a trip but I do remember years ago back-packing around Europe. I boarded a train to Budapest and found a man sitting in my seat. I was annoyed but took the seat opposite. He started talking to me and it turned out he was from Madrid and travelling too. We got on like a house on fire, hanging out together for the next month. We were so busy, I didn't really take in many of the places we visited.

Woman: Ah, that's a shame. It must have felt like a bit of a wasted trip.

Man: I wouldn't go that far. We kept in contact, and through him I learned some Spanish, which has helped me immensely over the years.

Narrator: Extract 3. You hear two friends discussing a travel trend called 'glamping', a style of camping.

Woman: I've recently been hearing a lot about glamping, but I'm still a bit confused about what it actually is. I mean I get that it's for people who like the great outdoors but don't want to rough it too much, but I'm not sure what makes it different to other types of camping. So, does it have to be under canvas or does it include things like tree houses? Anyway, you'd think it'd be cheaper than, say, a hotel but some of the popular sites actually cost more. Would you go glamping, Caleb?

Man: Mm, never say never, but it's not something I have a burning desire to do.

Woman: Why not?

Man: Well, I think it's a bit of a gimmick. Camping was the only cheap holiday at one time and now they've slapped a fancy label on it and suddenly, it's the same price as a hotel. I do like the look of some of the yurts – you know those cool, round tents and some of them are in stunning locations, but still. I'm not prepared to pay through the nose to stay in one. I'd rather go somewhere genuinely luxurious if I had enough cash.

Writing Part 2

1
1 People who are thinking of travelling to Amsterdam or other European cities
2 To help them evaluate/choose an online travel guide to use
3 Yes

2
1 C **2** E **3** B **4** D **5** A

3
1 landing page
2 click through
3 homepage
4 navigation
5 (options) menu
6 sidebar
7 link
8 blog
9 scroll down

Reading and use of English Part 5

1 B **2** D **3** A **4** C **5** A **6** B

Unit 12 Our planet

Vocabulary

1
1 depend on
2 apologise for
3 are/have been incorporated into
4 focus/are focusing on
5 protesting against
6 applied to
7 insisted on
8 attached to
9 contribute to

2
1 honoured
2 birdwatching
3 investigation
4 correct
5 city-dwelling
6 outdoors
7 firsthand
8 eye-witnesses
9 rip-off
10 correct
11 high-profile

Grammar

1
2 Ø **3** Ø **4** Ø **5** the **6** An **7** the **8** the
9 a **10** the **11** a **12** Ø **13** a/the **14** an

2
1 advice
2 information
3 correct
4 correct
5 bread
6 correct
7 baggage
8 correct
9 correct
10 damage

Writing Part 2

2
1 In recent years
2 of
3 Therefore
4 Similarly
5 In exchange
6 in order to
7 In addition
8 During

3
1 B **2** D **3** A **4** E **5** C

4
1 will co-ordinate/will be provided/will invite/will be made
2 going to invite
3 If my proposal is accepted, I will partner…
4 will be cleaning
5 can be made

5
1 assets
2 lay out
3 conservation
4 enhance
5 funding
6 operations
7 undertake
8 ownership

Listening Part 2

1 garden centre
2 internships
3 environmental protection
4 primates
5 monkey house
6 humidity
7 communication
8 websites

Track 13

Narrator: You will hear a conservationist called Emma Bradshaw giving a talk to a group of students on career opportunities in wildlife conservation. For questions 1–8, complete the sentences with a word or short phrase.

Emma: Hi, I'm Emma Bradshaw and I'm here to talk to you about careers in wildlife conservation. First off, this is a very competitive field. If you are passionate about wildlife conservation, it is never too early to get involved in working with the natural world. I, for example, did work experience at an animal rescue centre and helped out at the stables where I rode horses. Then, when I was doing my degree, I spent time in a garden centre, watering the plants and looking after the fish.

Even then, starting a career in conservation can be hard. Some people are lucky and manage to enter through volunteer roles or summer jobs, but this is rarely the case. What helped me get a foot in the door, and which I would recommend, was doing internships. I did several of these, which helped me build up my skills, and it was through one of these that I got offered some part-time work which led to my future career.

Obviously, study is also key for a job in this field. Most candidates study subjects like biology and zoology and pick up more hands-on skills through different work placements. There is also an amazing vocational qualification in environmental protection that I've seen offered, which can lead to careers in green energy, forestry and so on for those with a less academic background.

Although I'm now based out in the field, it is virtually impossible to start with a paid role like this. Like most people, I started with a zoo-based job. My preference was to look after the primates, but I started off taking care of penguins. I hated feeding time as the fish absolutely stank, but you have to be flexible.

It is a good idea to stay with an organisation long term rather than making regular changes. It was four years before an opening in the monkey house became available. The zoo director gave me the job, knowing I'd prefer that to working in the aviary where there was also a vacancy. I spent five years with capuchins and marmosets and loved every minute of it.

It was through the zoo that I got the opportunity to work in the field. I spent a year in Gabon, Central Africa, working on a project to reintroduce gorillas into the wild. It was fascinating, though living right in the middle of the rainforest miles from anywhere had its challenges: the accommodation was basic and it wasn't nice not having working showers or toilets. But that was nothing compared to the humidity. I just couldn't cope with that.

Remember, you can also contribute through jobs that indirectly support wildlife conservation. One of the fastest growing career paths is communication. We need people who can spread the word about environmentally friendly practices and our fund-raising efforts. Whatever skills you have, we can use them in the field of conservation.

People contribute most by doing what they do best, even if these are things you do for fun. For example, if you are an avid user of social media or write blog posts, you could administer websites for conservation groups. I really appreciate people with this talent as I'm a bit of a technophobe.

Reading and Use of English Part 7

1 G **2** A **3** E **4** C **5** D **6** F
B is not needed

Unit 13 A healthy lifestyle

Vocabulary

1
2 with **3** of **4** of **5** to **6** with **7** to **8** to **9** about **10** of **11** of

2
1 familiar to	**6** responsible for
2 closed to	**7** sensitive to
3 suited to	**8** frustrated about
4 delighted about/with/by	**9** acceptable to
5 confident about/of	

3
2 Correct	**6** kind to
3 anxious about	**7** confident of
4 suited to	**8** tolerant of
5 Correct	

Grammar

1
1 despite	**6** though
2 Even though	**7** While
3 Despite	**8** However
4 whereas	**9** Although
5 but	

2
2 All my family suffer from allergies. However, I seem to have escaped.
3 While Sofia enjoys skiing holidays, Delfina prefers lying on the beach. / Sofia enjoys skiing holidays, while Delfina prefers lying on the beach.
4 Despite being 95 years old, my grandmother still does her own housework.
5 My sister has asthma but it's not as bad as it used to be.
6 Colin and Jill live in the countryside. They go to London every week, though.
7 Even though I had a nice hot bath last night, my muscles ache.
8 Whereas Alfredo is extroverted, his sister Catherine is introverted. / Alfredo is extroverted, whereas his sister Catherine is introverted.
9 Although I take vitamins every day, I still catch a lot of colds.

3
2 My house isn't as well designed as yours.
3 We get fewer days off than other employees.
4 Emilie doesn't do as many activities as her sister.
5 This book is becoming more and more interesting.
6 Simon is by far the best skier in the team.
7 The second TV series is not nearly as funny as the first.
8 Tracey is more of an expert than me.
9 Jake makes less effort than the other students.

4
2 The north of Scotland is ~~by~~ far colder than the south of England.
3 It is much ~~more~~ better to give than to receive.
4 Children today don't have as ~~much~~ **many** books as children in the past (did).
5 This is the ~~worse~~ **worst** birthday I've ever had!
6 Correct
7 The winters are getting ~~more and more hot~~ **hotter and hotter** every year.
8 Running isn't **nearly as good** for you as swimming.
9 Correct

Reading and Use of English Part 3

1 EXCESSIVE
2 BASIS
3 OWNERSHIP
4 PRESSURE
5 UNTHINKABLE
6 CLARITY
7 COMMITMENTS
8 INCREDIBLY

Listening Part 3

1 B **2** C **3** B **4** D **5** D **6** B

Track 14	
Narrator:	You will hear an interview in which two practitioners of holistic well-being called Shalini Anand and Darren Peterson are talking about their work. Choose the answer (A, B, C or D) which fits best according to what you hear.
Interviewer:	Today we're talking to two practitioners of holistic well-being, Shalini Anand and Darren Peterson. Welcome, both of you. Shalini, can we start by clarifying what is meant by holistic well-being? Some of our listeners were wondering if it relates to alternative medicine, so things like homeopathy.
Shalini:	That's a fair question and it can be a bit confusing. Certainly, many alternative systems of medicine go back a long way and are based on the idea of different aspects of a person being interconnected. Modern holistic well-being embraces those ideas. While not necessarily advocating any particular system of alternative medicine, we base our approach on the understanding that different elements of a person and their way of life need to be in balance.
Interviewer:	OK, so you've referred a couple of times to the different aspects or elements of well-being. Can you explain what they are and how they relate to each other?
Shalini:	You often hear people talk about mind, body and spirit being the three aspects and then some add a fourth element, which is the social. But nowadays in holistic well-being, we talk about the five pillars of well-being, which are mental, emotional, physical, spiritual and social well-being. Some practitioners will lump mental and emotional well-being together, though it's not a view that I fully agree with. Most medics now acknowledge the physical and mental but the others are still neglected. The spiritual element is the one that even so-called holistic practitioners tend to leave aside as it is so deeply personal.

Interviewer:	Maybe you could say a little bit about the relationship between holistic and conventional approaches to medicine?
Shalini:	Holistic medicine is not generally viewed as an alternative to more established medical treatments but as complementary. So you might get pills from your doctor and then go to a holistic practitioner, who is not licensed to practise medicine, for hypnotherapy, for example. Having said that, like many of my colleagues, I am a fully qualified and practising general practitioner. My interest in holistic medicine developed as a result of my role. In fact this is a growing trend and has contributed to holistic treatments being viewed with less scepticism by the medical establishment.
Interviewer:	So, let's bring Darren in here. Shalini has explained to us what she means by holistic well-being. So, I suppose the question on all our minds now, is how can we achieve it?
Darren:	Well, small changes, like getting enough sleep and doing exercise do help, though they aren't enough on their own. We need to be kind to ourselves. Society often sets impossible standards for everything – like the clash between being a parent and doing a full-time job. It is so easy to think of ourselves as falling short in almost every way, especially in a world where we're constantly sharing images of ourselves in our best light. Give yourself a break. Have a mantra, such as 'You are good enough' and repeat it over and over.
Interviewer:	Um, good advice. And is there any specific advice you can give people related to well-being.
Darren:	Well, eat as healthily as you can but be wary of unrealistic and expensive trends. Take the craze for so-called superfoods for example. They do have high levels of nutrients but so do other less exotic, more accessible foods. Let's take the goji berry. They are full of antioxidants, but they are native to Asia, not Europe. People can live to be 100 without even hearing of a goji berry – by eating all kinds of fruit and vegetables which are grown close to where they live.
Interviewer:	That's fascinating. So, finally, Darren. Why should people take their holistic well-being seriously?
Darren:	Good question. I know a lot of people think it's just a fad but in fact it's been around forever. Let's take my grandmother as an example, who incidentally lived to be 102. Although she never heard of holistic well-being, when I think about her life, she was 'well' in terms of each of the five pillars Shalini mentioned. She walked everywhere because she was too poor to own a car, she had a wide circle of friends and was very accepting of everything life dealt her so had positive thinking in spades. I suppose her life is evidence of the need for holistic well-being.

Writing Part 2

1
2 promote
3 student body
4 implemented
5 refer you to
6 be an absolute priority

7 alarming
8 rethinking
9 a wider variety
10 I appreciate

2
Firstly – to begin with
Given – bearing in mind
To be frank – frankly
as a result – consequently
What is more – in addition
such as – including
In this way – this will mean that
Since – now that

Unit 14 A new land

Vocabulary

1
2 Incredibly, Adriana got the highest mark in the test.
3 Personally, I think young people shouldn't/don't think young people should be allowed to drive until the age of 18.
4 Apparently, the new building in town is going to be a sports centre.
5 Fortunately, the weather forecast is good for Kirsty and Dan's wedding day.
6 Undoubtedly, the strike by air traffic controllers will close the airport.
7 Wisely, Jamie decided not to drive in these icy conditions.
8 Melanie was absolutely devastated when she found out she'd failed her driving test.
9 To be honest, I'm sick of Brooke's behaviour.

2
1 offer
2 provided
3 offers
4 gave

5 gave/offered
6 provide
7 offered
8 provides

Grammar

1
2 What I want to know is how many people end up returning to their home country.
3 I do like Florence but I wish there were fewer tourists.
4 My mum wants all her children to be happy.
5 The place where we were happiest was Brighton.
6 The police chief himself came out to welcome us.
7 It is those who have lost their homes that I feel sorry for.
8 The news was so shocking that everyone was silent for several minutes.
9 The only thing I want (to do) is to go home and get into bed.

2
2 Why I asked about the car **is** because I might be interested in buying it.
3 Correct
4 One thing you could do to help is stack the chairs.
5 The president **herself** gave out the awards/gave out the rewards herself.
6 What I **believe** is that everyone has their own unique talents.
7 Correct
8 **The person who** started all the problems was Tyler.
9 Rarely **have** I seen so many elephants in one herd**.**
10 All ~~what~~ I need is enough money to live on.
11 Correct

Writing Part 1

1
1 Sasha
2 Martina
3 Martina
4 Carlos/Martina
5 Sasha/Martina

2
Carlos' introduction is the best. He starts with general sentences introducing the trend and mentions the two reasons he is going to discuss.

3

From the time of the industrial revolution, people have been migrating towards big cities in search of jobs, education and a better way of life. However, in recent decades, there have been signs of a reversal of this trend, with people moving to the countryside. In this essay, I will discuss what I **believe** are two of the main reasons for this: the pace of life and crime.

I **am of the view that** it is the desire for a slower pace of life that is the main driver of migration towards village and rural areas. While the fast-paced city lifestyle might suit the young, it is less popular with those raising families and older adults. **In my experience**, people have more time for each other in the countryside. They are more likely to stop for a chat and to help their neighbours, which, **to my mind**, raises the overall quality of life.

I **would also suggest that** high crime rates influence many people's decisions to move out of cities. **I am in no doubt that** older people, who are more vulnerable to crime as well as parents seeking to protect their children, see crime as the biggest disadvantage of city life. Both while at home and out and about, there is a lower chance of being a victim of theft or violent crime.

In conclusion, **I am convinced that** the more relaxed pace of life and safer streets are two reasons why people are choosing to leave over-populated urban areas in favour of more rural places.

4
1 In my opinion, I think that polluted air affects young children the most.
2 I agree with that the countryside is a better place to raise a family.
3 It is clearly clear that pollution levels are continuing to rise.
4 As far as I am concerned, cities are too dangerous for elderly people.
5 Absolutely I am **absolutely** sure that pollution is the main reason for people to leave cities.
6 In my point of view/**From** my point of view, the fast pace of life causes stress.

Reading and Use of English Part 6

1 A   2 C   3 C   4 D

Listening Part 4

Task One
(Distractors given in brackets)
1 F (A, C, G)
2 E (A, C, D, G)
3 B (A, E, G, H)
4 G (F, H)
5 H (C, D, E)

Task Two
(Distractors given in brackets)
6 G (F)
7 C (G, H)
8 F (C, G)
9 H (F, G)
10 B (H)

Track 15

Narrator: You will hear five short extracts in which people are talking about how their way of speaking has changed after moving abroad. For questions 1–5, choose from the list (A–H) the main reason the speaker gives for how the way they speak has developed. For questions 6–10, choose from the list (A–H) how each speaker feels about the way they now speak.

1
Man: I first came to Germany to work about ten years ago. The workforce at my company were pretty international so everyone tended to use English. I was keen to learn German so I went out of my way to interact with German speakers socially; however, since they were all so amazing at English, I didn't pick much up. I suppose I've got to where I am now through having the news on the TV every evening and downloading podcasts for my drive to work. Because I've learnt in a passive way, it stresses me out when I have to talk to people I don't know and my pronunciation could do with a boost.

2
Man: I was rubbish at languages at school, so didn't really expect to learn a language like Korean, which is totally unrelated to English. I initially came to Seoul for a year to help with English at a middle school and no-one is more astonished than me that I can actually hold a conversation in Korean now. The way Koreans react when they hear me speak their language never gets old. They're so impressed! I'm often asked what was so different about my experience of learning Korean and learning French at school. Clearly, I'm not a natural linguist but I have felt so warmly welcomed by Koreans and have had the time of my life here.

3
Woman: My family emigrated to Liverpool from Poland when I was eight. Unlike others who moved here at around the same age, I haven't lost my accent. The Liverpool accent known as 'Scouse' is supposed to be quite contagious, so people are often shocked when they hear how long I've been here. I put it down to the close bond I had with my extended family back home. I went back every summer and would sing traditional songs with my grandparents and run around the village with my cousins, enjoying a carefree existence. I do like the Scouse way of talking but I'm not at all bothered that I still sound Polish.

4
Woman: I'm a nurse and from the day I arrived here in New Zealand from Brazil I was with colleagues and patients who had strong Kiwi accents, so I 'caught' the accent that way, though, to a lesser extent, it was from watching local TV stations. Anyone I talk to just assumes I was born here, but I actually didn't move here until I was in my teens. When I go back to Brazil on holiday and for whatever reason I need to speak English, I feel a bit self-conscious. People think I'm putting on the accent to show off, which couldn't be further from the truth. It really bugs me.

5
Man: We've lived in Spain for seven years now. My wife and I retired here because of the weather. We're very settled here and do make a lot of effort to meet the locals. We even take classes at a language school, but we're stuck in the beginners' class. I'm forgetful even in English so I think I've left it too late. I still feel quite red-faced about not having learnt more of the language of these lovely, hospitable people. It really irritates me when younger people who live here don't bother to learn Spanish. I do try to use the few words I know, such as 'hola' or 'gracias' and even that much is appreciated.

Reading and Use of English Part 4

1 are prohibited from taking
2 not have objected to
3 face the music if I'm/I am
4 has been suffering from
5 as/so much pleasure in gardening as
6 have I been spoken to so/has anyone spoken to me so

Acknowledgements

The authors and publishers acknowledge the following sources of copyright material and are grateful for the permissions granted. While every effort has been made, it has not always been possible to identify the sources of all the material used, or to trace all copyright holders. If any omissions are brought to our notice, we will be happy to include the appropriate acknowledgements on reprinting and in the next update to the digital edition, as applicable.

Key: U = Unit

Photography

All the photographs are sourced from Getty Images.

U1: Oliver Rossi/Stone; Mayur Kakade/Moment; Ryan McVay/The Image Bank; **U2:** Nattakorn Maneerat/iStock/Getty Images Plus; d3sign/Moment; Kelvin Murray/Stone; **U3:** Compassionate Eye Foundation/Robert Daly/OJO Images/Stone; skynesher/E+; Valeriy_G/iStock/Getty Images Plus; **U4:** Juan Jose Napuri/iStock/Getty Images Plus; sanjeri/E+; Ariel Skelley/DigitalVision; **U5:** GoodLifeStudio/E+; Georgette Douwma/Stone; Terry Vine/The Image Bank; kali9/E+; **U6:** Neustockimages/E+; Thomas Barwick/Stone; **U7:** kali9/E+; SDI Productions/E+; Tim Robberts/DigitalVision; **U8:** tomazl/iStock/Getty Images Plus; vm/E+; Aja Koska/E+; **U9:** Nick David/Stone; seregalsv/iStock/Getty Images Plus; HRAUN/E+; **U11:** vidalidali/iStock/Getty Images Plus; monkeybusinessimages/iStock/Getty Images Plus; **U12:** Mark Newman/The Image Bank; Илија Симевски/500Px Plus; Martin Harvey/The Image Bank; Frank and Helena/Image Source; **U13:** Moyo Studio/E+; Wachirawut Priamphimai/EyeEm; AscentXmedia/E+; Yellow Dog Productions/The Image Bank; svetikd/iStock/Getty Images Plus; **U14:** David C Tomlinson/The Image Bank; Thomas Barwick/DigitalVision.

Cover photography by BackyardProduction/iStock/Getty Images Plus/Getty Images.

Audio

Audio production by Leon Chambers.

Typesetting

Typesetting by Hyphen S.A.